T0339823

A DIMLY BURNING WICK

A DIMLY BURNING WICK

MEMOIR FROM THE RUINS OF HIROSHIMA

by Sadako Teiko Okuda

with Pamela Bea Wilson Vergun

With contributions by:
Ronald Takaki
Paul Joseph
Pamela Vergun and Robert Vergun
Catherine Thomasson
Martin Donohoe
Sok-Hon Ham, Nobel Peace Prize nominee

Illustrated by Mia Nolting

Algora Publishing
New York

Library of Congress Cataloging-in-Publication Data —

Okuda, Sadako.
   [Honogurai tooshin o kesu koto naku. English]
   A dimly burning wick: memoir from the ruins of Hiroshima / by Sadako
Teiko Okuda; with Pamela Bea Wilson Vergun; with contributions by Ronald
Takaki ... [et al.] ; illustrated by Mia Nolting.
      p. cm.
   Includes bibliographical references.
   ISBN 978-0-87586-560-7 (soft: alk. paper) — ISBN 978-0-87586-561-4
(hard cover: alk. paper) — ISBN 978-0-87586-562-1 (ebook) 1. Hiroshima-
shi (Japan)—History—Bombardment, 1945—Personal narratives. 2. Okuda,
Sadako. 3. Atomic bomb victims—Japan—Hiroshima-shi. I. Title.

   D767.25.H6O4613 2008
   940.54'2521954092—dc22
   [B]
                                        2007052058

Front Cover:

Printed in the United States

Hono gurai tooshin o kesu koto naku.
"A dimly burning wick He will not quench."
—Isaiah 42: 3

Japanese calligraphy by Umeko Masumoto

I dedicate this work to the children and adults who suffered, and in some cases even survived, with grace the terror and heartbreak of Hiroshima and Nagasaki, the Bravo Test, slavery, and the Holocaust, and all those whose hearts have withered or perished in other disasters large and small. May their memories be for a blessing.

And to my family — my Miko and Isaac, their "Grandma" and "Papa," and my Rob — my partner and my love. Without their support and hope for the future this book might not have come into being.

TABLE OF CONTENTS

FOREWORD

To understand the nuclear devastation of Hiroshima, few things are more powerful than first-hand accounts. In the case of *A Dimly Burning Wick*, the overwhelming horror accompanies uplifting moments of hope, generosity, and caring that have the power to lead us further from nuclear weapons and war.

Many people around the world and Americans in particular have never been to a war zone; very few who are alive now have actually witnessed the devastation caused by a nuclear bomb. This book will help bring to the reader a more realistic understanding and abhorrence of the tools of war, above all nuclear weapons. All of us, I believe, have the opportunity and duty to achieve the abolition of nuclear weapons.

Bombs — even "only" conventional ones — not only kill and maim but also destroy a society's infrastructure, its hospitals, bridges, businesses, and schools. Their use runs the risk of creating failed states. When such undiscriminating weapons are used, civilians of the targeted societies are alienated and become more militant. As we enter the 21st century, approximately 90% of the casualties (killed or wounded) in war are civilians.[1] This statistic, which shows that war is targeting

---

[1] Kaldor, Mary (2003) "Beyond Militarism, Arms Races and Arms Control," in Geir Lundestad and Olav Njolstad (eds.) *War and Peace in the 20th Century and Beyond*, World Scientific Publishing Company, p. 159.

not soldiers but rather other adults and children, should help all of us to resist governments' use of war as a foreign policy strategy — it is those of us who are not soldiers who are most likely to die as the result of war. There is no glory in "shock and awe"; we have only to look at Afghanistan and Iraq to see this. How can we avoid this type of warfare from this point forward, whether carried out by nations or by individuals taking up weapons?

My perspective as a physician helps me to see the parallels between war and what we conventionally think of as disease. I view war as a disease to be prevented, and the United Nations in the aftermath of World War II emerged as a promising tool to prevent this disease. Yet, prevention also requires that nations respect and strengthen international law and truly commit to the use of peacekeeping forces when needed. In addition, the prevention of war, like any disease, requires the world community to address the root causes: conditions such as poverty, inequality, and the scarcity of valuable resources such as water, oil, and farmland — the unmet needs of people. It also requires us to build peace by using nonviolence and cooperation as organizing principles.

In first-world[2] countries in particular, the prevention of war requires the facilitation of a more responsible and sometimes circumspect media, and attention to accurate portrayals of opponents, rather than the prevalent tendency to demonize the enemy. In collusion with the media, many governments (including the US) keep the experiences and pictures of war from reaching the average citizen. This allows governments to make war seem justified and hide the humanity of those hurt by war.

There are more effective ways to achieve foreign and domestic policy goals than aggressive military action. Unfortunately, some leaders currently suggest that being the first in a conflict to use nuclear weapons is a "legitimate" approach. Some senior NATO military leaders are now advocating this position; for example, they propose explod-

---

2 Though not as often used as "third world", the term "first-world countries" refers to countries that are democracies, that are technologically advanced, and many of whose citizens have a relatively high standard of living.

ing nuclear weapons on a country to stop it from continuing to build nuclear weapons.[3]

In short, preventing war requires citizens to join our voices to effectively counteract attempts by our leaders — for any reason — to advocate war and the actions that lead us to it.

Today the stakes continue to rise. The increased power of advanced nuclear weapons combined with the sheer number available for use makes clear the wisdom of Martin Luther King, Jr.'s words with which this book ends: It is either nonviolence or nonexistence. No other weapon matches the ability of nuclear weapons to devastate and destroy. As much as some might want to think otherwise, nuclear weapons are essentially instruments of terror. They threaten indiscriminate violence on the most extreme scale. It is no wonder that in 1996 the International Court of Justice declared the use and even the threat to use nuclear weapons illegal by international law.

Very few people even know that there are over 27,000 nuclear weapons worldwide. Most of the nations that hold nuclear weapons have signed the nuclear Non-Proliferation Treaty (NPT), obligating those nations to begin the process of abolishing these weapons.[4] The treaty is essentially a bargain between those nations with nuclear weapons, who have promised to get rid of them, and those without, who have vowed never to acquire them in exchange for nuclear-related information and technology. In spite of the dark side of this treaty, the incorrect assumption that nuclear technology once received would do no harm (Eisenhower's naïve "Atoms for Peace" plan), the treaty contains in Article VI the only existing legally-binding international and explicit commitment to nuclear disarmament: "Each of the Parties to

---

3 Naumann, Klaus, John Shalikashvili, Peter Inge, Jacques Lanxade, and Henk van den Breemen (2007) *Towards a Grand Strategy for an Uncertain World: Renewing Transatlantic Partnership*, Noaber Foundation.

4 See Cirincione, Joseph, Jon Wolfsthal, and Miriam Rajkumar (2005) *Deadly Arsenals: Nuclear, Biological, and Chemical Threats*, Second Edition Revised and Expanded, Carnegie Endowment for International Peace. Some of the data in the report are originally from *The Bulletin of Atomic Scientists*. See also Norris, Robert S., Hans M. Kristensen, and Christopher E. Paine (2004) *Nuclear Insecurity: A Critique of the Bush Administration's Nuclear Weapons Policies*, National Resource Defense Council. Nuclear nations who have signed the NPT are the US, Russia, UK, France, and China. Between 210 and 310 nuclear weapons are in the possession of India, Israel, and Pakistan, who have not signed the NPT.

the Treaty undertakes to pursue negotiations in good faith... on a treaty on general and complete disarmament under strict and effective international control."

Despite Article VI, the five major nuclear states that have signed the treaty have not seriously worked toward dismantling their systems, despite the blueprint for action put in place by the 2000 Review Conference of the NPT. Furthermore, the United States in 2005 worked to obstruct the proceedings of the Review Conference of the NPT, undermining progress.

In response to this situation, there has been a greater call for disarmament. Numerous leaders, including former Secretaries of State Henry Kissinger and George Shultz, have called for a bold new vision: a world free of nuclear weapons.[5] International Physicians for the Prevention of Nuclear War has instituted the International Campaign to Abolish Nuclear Weapons (ICAN) in order to build a global citizens' movement with the help of Non-Governmental Organizations and to push for progressive negotiations that will achieve the abolition of nuclear weapons. This will provide for the elimination of nuclear weapons, similar to treaties that have banned landmines as well as chemical and biological weapons. Already in existence is the technology to provide effective means to verify compliance. The majority of United Nations member states have called for negotiations on a nuclear weapons convention that would abolish nuclear weapons, consistent with the goal of ICAN.

As we move farther away in history from the bombing of Hiroshima and Nagasaki, it is human nature to want to forget the horrific effects of the nuclear bombs dropped on those cities. This book brings the past directly back in view and puts human faces on the appalling deaths. It allows us to feel the pain of those horrendous burns and the terror of radiation sickness.

In this global age, we must recognize our interdependence if we are to survive. Young and old, we all hold the responsibility to bear witness to the voices of the children of Hiroshima and Nagasaki. Their experiences must remain alive in our collective memory, like the light

---

5 Shultz, George, William Perry, Henry Kissinger, and Sam Nunn (January 4, 2007) "Toward a Nuclear-Free World," *Wall Street Journal*, p. A15.

from a dimly burning wick that can illumine the darkness and yet must be carefully protected from being extinguished. Just as the children sought to keep the vulnerable flickering flames of the people they loved alight, so can we follow their example in protecting others and in doing so protect our earth and its invaluable resources. The key to this is understanding the interdependency of humankind.

Seeing war through the eyes of children should awaken in us all the fervor to find new means to resolve international and civil conflicts. We need more books like this one to inspire world citizens to work with organizations that are striving to abolish nuclear weapons. I am honored to write a foreword for this remarkable book, which is a wonderful resource for raising our awareness of why abolition is vital. My hope for you is that reading this book will move you to help achieve one of the greatest civil rights goals imaginable, the abolition of nuclear weapons.

Catherine Thomasson, MD
Past President of Physicians for Social Responsibility

Message from the Author upon the Publication of Her Book in English

Now that I am 93 years old, the words I have written are reaching outside the region of the world where I live.

I want you to know how much I believe in world peace. I hope that this book will touch many hearts from many countries and belief systems.

I wish that all peoples will work so that there will be no more war like the one I experienced. I also want you to know how much I regret that Japan started the war.

May you have the blessings of peace and of knowing that you too through your actions have worked to bring peace.

Sadako Okuda

In the Beginning

August 6, 1945

The morning the atomic bomb was dropped, I was on Osaki-shimo Island, a quiet island in the Inland Sea off Hiroshima. Even though I was sixty kilometers away from the city, it was clear that something horrific had happened.

Early that morning, I happened to go to the hospital clinic. Although the doctors were all away at the front, you could still get shots from the matrons and nurses. I had just stuck out my arm, ready for a shot, when there was a blinding flash. I felt some pain in my head and neck as if a needle had pricked me. I was given the shot anyway and was about to head home when the tingling and prickling sensations in the right side of my neck increased in intensity. I found that my neck had been burned. It did not matter that I was several kilometers away from the site of the devastation — the blinding flash damaged my vision and hearing. My ability to see and hear continued to decline as the years passed.

After receiving treatment for the burn, I once again sat down on the chair I had been sitting on when the flash had hit me. I looked around — I did not understand what exactly had caused my neck injury. About a meter away from my seat was a window; the glass had broken and there was a hole in the windowpane. The hole in the glass had exactly the same shape as the burn I had sustained.

Soon a commotion arose throughout the village. The rumors that reached us were that Hiroshima was devastated — everyone was dead and all of the houses had burned down. Almost immediately, people in our village organized boats to help villagers go to Hiroshima to look for their family members who lived there. We heard that anyone who wanted to go should let the organizers know. After talking with my mother, I decided to join the group.

My older brother Yasutami lived in Hiroshima City but had been drafted to the front along with many brothers. However, his wife, Hanako, was still in Hiroshima taking care of their house. With her were their two small children. My niece, Fuyo-chan, was a sixth-grader and her brother, Yukiaki, a fourth-grader.

A close friend of our family, whom we called Uncle, also lived in the city in a house adjoining his pharmacy.

I was thirty years old that August, living with my mother on the island and teaching knitting to my young students. I was known affectionately as *Shima no Sensei*, Teacher of the Island. I had miraculously survived a several-year struggle with tuberculosis, which explains in part my petite frame and why I had never married.

I left for Hiroshima on the morning of August 7, arriving at the Port of Ujina at about noon. As the boat approached the wharf, the first evident sign of devastation was the sky, which was a threatening shade of dark red. Standing on the wharf, I did not know where I should go or how I should get there. But, because I had gone to school for many years in Hiroshima, I was able to locate my uncle's house. As I began to make my way through the town, I saw many injured people being carried toward the wharf.

Much like the other houses I passed, my uncle's house was half-destroyed. There I found my uncle, who had survived the blast. My brother's wife had found her way to my uncle's, but her children were missing. She had been trying to search for them, but the situation in Hiroshima was so terrible that she was unable to find them and was soon worn out in despair and extreme fatigue. I began searching for them throughout the city, using my uncle's house as a base.

The day of my arrival, I was terrified of everything I saw and heard. Covering my eyes and plugging my ears, I fled in bewilderment. Searching day after day near ground zero, my eyes grew red and weary. I called out the names of my niece and nephew in the neighborhood where they lived until my voice was hoarse. As I searched the devastated town, my clothes often caught fire and I would hurriedly put it out.

Each day before I resumed my search, my uncle, a pharmacist, gave me injections of vitamin B and C. He said, "You'll get worn out searching, so it might help — anyhow, it's better than nothing." In those days, that was about all there was in the pharmacy. I later learned that the shots had helped my body handle the radiation to which I had been exposed.

The eight days of my search for my niece and nephew were mercilessly long and filled with pain and sorrow — as well as rage. This is the story of the children, mothers, grandparents, and others whom I met during my long days of searching in Hiroshima.

OUR SHARED RESPONSIBILITY

During World War II, even the youngest child in Japan was forbidden to say anything against the fighting, no matter how painful things were. I am burdened with regret and frustration that I did not find a voice to speak out against the atrocities and the stupidity of war. My purpose now is to make up for all the years of silence.

I want to be able to reassure the children of today, those yet to come, and those who have died, "You can sleep peacefully, because we will not repeat this crime."[6] In the face of what happened in Hiroshima, *each of us* is entrusted with this heavy responsibility. My prayer is that I will never forget the gravity of this responsibility and that I can spend the rest of my days bearing witness to the truth.

I wonder if people realize how many victims of Hiroshima were not adults, but young children — how many were not even Japanese, but rather from countries like Korea.[7] I will do all I can to make up for the added injustice they have had to face.

The following account was extracted from my diary in which I described those days of searching. I wrote my diary in a notebook with rough paper and a pencil, and as a result, the pages of the notebooks became ragged, torn, and out of order. The diary is now little more than scraps of paper. There is a part of me that would like to burn my tattered notes once my story is published, just as the people of Hiroshima witnessed so much that was precious to them turned into ashes: their houses, their memories, and even their loved ones.

---

6 This alludes to the inscription on the memorial cenotaph located in Hiroshima Peace Park.

7 Before the end of the war, the Japanese government and its agents brought many Korean people to Japan as forced labor; others ended up in Japan after Japan's colonial takeover of Korea in 1910. Thus, at least 50,000 Koreans were in Hiroshima at the time of the bombing and/or were exposed to lethal levels of radiation in the period shortly afterwards. (Yoneyama, Lisa (1995) "Memory Matters: Hiroshima's Korean Atom Bomb Memorial and the Politics of Ethnicity," *Public Culture* vol. 7, issue 3, p. 502.) It is estimated that one in every seven victims of the atomic bombing of Hiroshima was Korean. See Hane, Mikiso (1992) *Modern Japan: A Historical Survey*, Westview Press. In addition, many American citizens of Japanese descent were visiting family and were trapped by the sudden outbreak of war. They also became A-bomb victims through American actions in August 1945. The plight of non-Japanese victims, especially those who have never received aid, many of them Korean, continues to be of concern.

But deep down, I realize that even if I physically burn the note-books, I will never be able to extinguish the memories that are seared into my consciousness and heart. Time does not heal my broken heart. In fact, the burn in my heart has become increasingly painful. I sincerely wish that as a result of reading this book, you too would pray for peace. These children should not have suffered the terrible sentence imposed for the Japanese people's actions in war.

The words for the title of this book, *A Dimly Burning Wick (He Will Not Quench)* are taken from Isaiah 40: 3. I wanted to convey my prayer for complete peace, so that there will be no more lives destroyed in vain — gone out like the light from a dimly burning wick.

If There Had Been No War...

"My son, no matter how much I taught you,
You couldn't say 'two.'
Finally yesterday you said it — 'Twwoo!' But...
'Mama, Mama,' you would say to me,
Always attached to your mother,
Never-separated boy.

"What terrible thing has happened to you?
I'm a bad mother, aren't I?
If you had been right beside your mother at that moment,
This wouldn't have happened...
Come here now — Mama will hold you.
You always like to take your naps like this, don't you?"

She took the boy's hand, which was burned and bloated,
And had grown cold,
Gently laying it on her breast.
She held him close,
As she would do when putting her boy to sleep.
Dissolving into tears, she rocked his body slowly, slowly.

The mother's tears fell
From her cheek to her chin and onto his face...
Though behind her and beside her was a sea of fire,
The mother couldn't move.
I, too, my tears rolling from cheek to chin,
Dropping onto the backs of my clenched hands.

The mother and I said, "If there had been no war..."
And we embraced each other,
Crying as we parted.
The mother firmly grasped my hands, saying,
"I've got to be strong. I must have the strength of two,
Because my boy's spirit is within me now."

As I reluctantly walked away, I would look back,
And again stop and wave.
Each time she would deeply bow her head to bid goodbye.
I would walk and again look back.
The mother was still there.
She will probably remain there forever.

The last time I looked, the mother
Was holding the boy, broken down, weeping.
Trying not to look back again,
Afraid to turn my head, I ran,
The sound of flames all around me,
The awful smell chasing me all the way.

Later, I returned to that place.
The mother had died, her son in her arms.
Human life can disappear like smoke.
So, even though she said all she had said to me,
About being strong —
Even so, this ended up being the outcome....

— Sadako Teiko Okuda

The Big Brother and Little Sister Who Waited

Afternoon, August 7, 1945

After arriving at my uncle's house in Hiroshima that morning, I prepared to search the city for my niece and nephew. I packed in my bag a few basic provisions: green tea, hand towels, rice balls, and a medicine called Mercurochrome. As I was starting on my way, my uncle said to me, "I think I may need to take a short rest. Come home as soon as you can, Sadako." I walked on, but found myself worrying about him and wondering if I should go back to care for him.

I was so wrapped up in my thoughts that I did not notice the distance I had walked. Sharply cutting into my thoughts came a young boy who veered into me on a bicycle. A little girl was sitting behind her brother on the bike, and before I could blink, she had fallen off. As I ran toward them, the young boy jumped off, threw the bike down, and frantically lifted up the little girl.

"Are you OK? Keiko! Keiko!" he called, but there was no reply — she didn't even open her eyes.

I took the girl from the anguished boy and tried slapping her cheeks and shaking her, but her eyes would not open and her body was completely still. I managed to detect a faint pulse. Still holding onto the little girl, I quickly got on the back of the bicycle, crying out to the boy, "Let's go! Go! Go! Hurry!"

The young boy jumped on the bicycle and pedaled furiously as I directed him toward my uncle's house. It must have been very hard for him, since the bicycle bore us as well. Occasionally he would stop and gasp in pain. When this happened, I would impatiently call out to him from behind, "Hurry! Hurry! Go!" my heart clanging like a fire bell.

We were not yet halfway to my uncle's house when the young boy suddenly stopped. "I'm sorry," he whispered. "Please get off. I can't go any more. Ah! It hurts.... It hurts.... I want a drink of water! Water..."

"Hang in there! How bad is the pain?" I asked as I quickly got off the bike, Keiko still in my arms. He shrugged his shoulders, but he looked half-dead. All the strength appeared to have left his body and his skin was deathly white. He looked like he was about to fall over any second. I held Keiko with one arm, and put my other arm around her brother and held him tightly.

The young boy collapsed into my arms. "I can't go any further," he cried out. "I can't even stand."

"Come on.... Hey! Look at me!" I urged him. He raised his eyes weakly.

"Water... Please give me some water," he moaned. "Let me have some water." He hung his tired little head.

I took out from my bag some green tea, and little by little, I poured some into his mouth. He swallowed about two mouthfuls, and, after a little while, he opened his mouth for more.

"Are you all right?" I asked. "I'm sorry.... I shouldn't have pushed you so." He laid his head in my lap to rest. I gently stroked his back. Gradually, he seemed to relax.

I was trying to stay calm for the sake of the boy and his sister, but I could not help but wonder what would become of these two. At that moment, I looked at his little sister. While I had been taking care of her older brother, Keiko-chan had traveled far away, where our hands could not reach. Our efforts were in vain; even though there had been a pulse... It was now too late. I felt completely weak. Keiko-chan's mouth was slightly open and blood was flowing steadily from her lips.

I silently begged this innocent little girl for forgiveness and caressed her tiny, darling hand. "Poor Keiko-chan, I didn't caress you even once. I'm so sorry." I did not want to wake the boy, so I quietly lowered him down to the ground for a moment while I gently laid his little sister not far away from him, and sheltered her face with my hat.

After a short while, the young boy stirred. Unaware of his sister's passing, he looked up at me and asked, "Excuse me, but if you have some medicine, can you please put some on me?"

I asked him where he wanted the medicine. Gingerly taking off his jacket, he let me see his back. I couldn't help but draw back in horror. I never could have imagined the gruesomeness of his injury. Extending from his left shoulder all the way down to his right hip, the boy's flesh had been gouged out, leaving a gaping open wound.

"Oh, my! Why didn't you say something *sooner*?" I was horrified. "When you were this badly wounded — what were you thinking of, trying to carry your little sister on your bike?"

"Mom was crushed under the house," he explained, "so we were on our way to see our aunt. But it doesn't matter. She may also be dead, for all I know." Tears were pouring from his eyes and he bit his lip in an effort to fight back the pain and the sorrow. I took a deep breath, put my arm around his back, and suggested that we continue on to my uncle's house, since the little bit of medicine I had with me would not be enough.

"How about it?" I asked. "Do you think you can walk?"

He lowered his head. "I can't go on," he replied. "I'll stay here. I'll be fine. Just let me lie here — I'll sleep here with my little sister. Thank you for all you have done."

He then let out a huge sigh and closed his eyes. I was at a total loss. My heart would not allow me to leave him alone with his dead sister, yet I knew that I still had to look for my brother's children. How could I leave this boy when he did not even know that his sister was no longer alive? There was no time to waste. I decided that I would run home and bring back some more medicine for the boy. I told him that, on the way, I would look for someone to help him until I returned.

I stroked his forehead. "Rest here for now, OK?"

He nodded obediently. "OK, I will."

Before I went on my way, I applied the rest of the medicine to his wound, thinking that it would be better than doing nothing. The sight of his wound made me feel queasy and sick to my stomach.

I was ashamed of my own weakness especially in the face of his bravery. He was clearly in a great deal of pain, but did not cry out as I applied the medicine. Gradually, though, his face grew pale, and an oily sweat trickled down his cheeks and neck. I was worried that he might lose consciousness. I wiped the sweat off with my hand towel, but new beads of sweat formed as soon as I wiped the old ones away.

I have to act quickly, I thought to myself. If I don't do something right away... It would be awful if this little one ends up dying as well. I began to tremble in fear.

I said to him, "I'll have to go home by myself to bring back some medicine and an injection of vitamin C. Do you think you can wait?"

Although he evidently was in pain, he replied in a clear voice, "Yes, I'll be waiting. Please take my bicycle."

I told the boy that I had never learned how to ride a bike, but reassured him that I did know how to *run* fast. The boy smiled weakly in gratitude.

I folded up the hand towel and gently put it under his head. Repeatedly, I assured him that I would return soon. "So don't go anywhere, OK?"

I took in my surroundings in search of a landmark that would help me find my way back here and came across a fallen sign from a nearby vegetable shop. I made a mental note of the sign and before heading out in the direction of my uncle's house, I returned to the boy's side once more. Even though I knew that there was no time to spare, I was frightened to leave the boy alone. "Are you all right?" I asked him. "I *will* come back. You *will* be waiting here, right?"

The young boy, now unable to move his head, grasped the bottom of my *mompé*[8] firmly. "I won't leave this place," he said. "I'll wait here forever. Please come back to me." Then he extended both hands toward me, asking again politely, "Excuse me, but could I have a little water?" I raised him up and gave him some more tea.

After helping him settle on the ground again, I began to run. I could not stop thinking about this intelligent-looking young boy with those imploring eyes that silently begged me not to leave him. One part of me believed that with such a significant wound, there was nothing to be done — and that my time would be better spent looking for my missing niece and nephew. Another part of me, though, was convinced that if

---

8 *Mompé* are pants typically worn by Japanese farmers. Resembling dark-colored sweat pants with elastic at the waist and ankles, *mompé* were traditionally worn by women doing farm work or other hard labor. *Mompé* became the requisite patriotic outfit of all Japanese women during the war, indicative of their frugality and practicality.

I was quick enough, I could somehow save the boy's life. While these thoughts raced through my head, I kept on running as fast as I could.

At one point, I stumbled over some debris and fell. My head swam. I realized I was lying on the ground, and I felt as if I were going to pass out any second. I could not afford to give in to the dizziness, so I picked myself up quickly and started on my way again. As I looked carefully about me, I saw that I had actually not come as far as I had thought.

I started to panic as I thought about the young boy. His bright eyes and pale face flashed across my mind. I became impatient and had to tell myself to calm down. After running for some time, I finally reached home, where my uncle was resting after having worked himself to the point of exhaustion.

While I had been away, several people had found refuge in my uncle's house. I was too distracted to tell anyone what had happened, and so I was expected to help out. People commented on how I absent-mindedly kept making mistakes, but I could not concentrate. My head was filled with images of the young boy and his poor sister.

Before I knew it, minutes turned into hours. Unable to stand the thought of the boy suffering out there any longer, I ran back to the boy at full speed, carrying whatever medicine I had managed to find. I do not remember seeing anything along the way — only the battered sign belonging to the vegetable shop.

From a distance, I saw the young boy lying on the ground. I ran over to him and looked down at the boy — now dead — and I squatted down, trembling. In my misery and sorrow, I bit my lip so hard that it bled. I cried out, sobbing, for the young boy who had died holding his little sister's hand.

I could not control the flow of tears. "I'm sorry! I should have come back more quickly!" I repeated the same words over and over again in deep remorse.

An old man had been sitting near the bodies of the two children. He came up to me and gently asked if I had known the young boy and his little sister. I could only shake my head in response; I was too heartbroken to speak.

"I came to search for my son's wife and my grandchild," the old soft-spoken man informed me. "But I have no idea where they are, and

I'm so tired of walking and trying to find them. How impossible it is even to think of finding our own loved ones among so many dead! How terrible!"

The old man was thinking of giving up and going home. He had walked around all day, calling out their names until he was hoarse, but they were not to be found and the situation seemed more and more hopeless as time passed. As he spoke, he gazed up at the sky.

"Let's go home for today," he said, "and look for our loved ones tomorrow. Shall I try one more day?"

"I wonder," he continued, as if speaking to himself. "Did my grandchild die hating war, as this brother and sister here did? This boy died bearing a bitter grudge against war, and against adults. He said that the adults made the war without thinking of us — the adults cheated us — they told us that Japan would definitely win the war. They tricked us, he said. This boy was right. Children aren't to blame for the war. Those poor little ones! When I think that my grandchild, too, might have died saying such things, I feel my heart breaking. It must be true that we adults are bad. How can it be that children have died in such a brutal way, though they bear no guilt? We adults need to learn to be like these innocent children."

Up to only a few days before, it was inconceivable that someone would give voice to these thoughts.

The old man then stretched out both arms, as if he were yearning for something, so I let him hold the little girl in his arms for a few minutes. His hands, wrinkled with age, wiped the sweat and the tears from his coal-black, dirty face.

"It's inhuman. It's repulsive to me to live even one day more in a world like this," he wailed.

I looked at the dead boy lying on the ground. I did not know his name or anything about him. I searched to see if he had something that would identify him, but found nothing except for a portion of his identification tag that remained on his chest. It only said, *Classroom 2.*"

As for the little sister, the name *Keiko* was written on her small, handmade satchel. Inside the satchel, there was a handkerchief that had been made by cutting a hand towel in half, along with some coarse black tissues that had been carefully folded. The little finger of her left hand had been badly burned.

"I'm sorry. I know that no matter how much I apologize, it won't do any good," I told her as I applied medicine to her finger. Nonetheless, I continued to apply the rest of the medicine and bandaged her finger, then crossed her hands on her chest. Her fingernails were cut neatly. I tried to block from my mind the image of the children's mother chatting lovingly with them as she trimmed their nails.

I laid the two children down next to each other and wrote a note to leave by them: *Please cremate these two together.*

The sunset was beautiful, and I thought how wonderful it would be if there were not such sorrow in the world — if there were peace now! I imagined how, if there were no such violence and fear, these two would be with their mother right now.

I was about to leave for home when the old man gently laid them in my lap and said, "Hold them for a little while, since they were waiting so."

Looking into the boy's face, I said, "Little One, you waited, didn't you? You waited here, asking the old man where I was. You said to him, 'I hope she will come soon.' Little One, I was late, but I'm here now. Little One, please let me hug you." Holding him tightly in my arms, I wanted to shout as he had, "*Stupid* war!" The tragedy was that I was too afraid as an adult to say those words.

Once I was back at the house, I described my day to my uncle while washing the dishes. My uncle quietly commented that he was glad he was unable to go to war. "I shudder to think of the pain and sorrow I would have inflicted," he said. As he got up to go to bed, my uncle patted my shoulder and advised me, "Go to bed early. You will want to go and search again tomorrow."

As I finished cleaning up, I didn't know what to do about the sorrow rising within me. I returned to my room and when I sat down quietly on my bed, I could still feel the weight of their bodies in my lap. Over and over again, I asked for their forgiveness. "I'm sorry.... I'm so sorry," I repeated.

That evening, the sky was beautiful. It was hard to imagine how the world could be so full of sadness when there was such quiet and serene beauty. That night two more tiny stars were added to Heaven.

WHERE HAS YUUICHI GONE?

That night while I slept, I was haunted by the face and voice of a little boy from another family, Yuuichi, whom I had met that afternoon.

The boy had told me of his grandfather. "When my Papa left for war, Papa told me to make sure that Grandpa eats, even if I have to skip a meal. But Grandpa always says, 'I'm not hungry — you can have the rest of mine.'"

The boy continued, "Yesterday Grandpa said his back was hurting when he had to push our cart. He asked me to help, but I told him I was tired and I'd help him tomorrow. Grandpa went on, rubbing his aching back.

"At night when I was hot, Grandpa moistened his hand towel and used it to cool me off. 'There, that must feel nice,' he sighed, as though he wished someone were there to help him wash the sweat off his own skin.

"Grandpa would scratch my itchy places with his hands, gritty from all the work he does. 'Yuu, does that feel better?'

"When I told Grandpa to buy me new sneakers, Grandpa flinched, but then gently answered, 'Yes, Yuuichi, I will when I make some money.' He patted me on the head and smiled down at me."

As I slept that night, I remembered how Yuuichi that afternoon had buried his face against the back of his grandpa, sobbing. "WHY DID YOU DIE AND LEAVE ME? Grandpa, our house burnt down, and your cart caught fire. What should Yuu do from now on? I don't understand how I'm supposed to live..."

And then, lost in thought, the boy said in a small voice, "Grandpa, you often said, didn't you, that you wanted to go somewhere where there is no war."

I told the boy, "I'll come back in a little while and then take you home with me." The little boy nodded his head emphatically. Completely quiet, he looked up at me. Unable to handle the situation, I remember telling him, "*Don't cry.* Stop it. Boys must be strong, remember?" I placed a rice ball in his hand. The little boy nodded and looked up at me again. His face was scrunched up, stained with dirt and tears. He tried to conceal his pain, as I had asked.

I left to search for my family and when I returned later that afternoon to get him, both the grandpa and the boy were gone. Grandpa's stained hand towel and one of the Grandpa's straw thongs were there, both smoldering.... I sank down weakly, lacking the strength to search for them.

I too want to go somewhere where there is no war. I asked the smoldering thong, "Why can't I — why can't we — yell this from the roof tops?"

The image of Yuuichi's face as he told the story of his Grandpa will forever haunt my dreams: a little boy with a small voice, holding steadfastly onto the rice ball, holding back his sadness as I walked away.

Masako-chan, Who Couldn't See

Morning, August 8, 1945

Even though it had been only 24 hours since I left my home on the island, my body and soul were exhausted; I felt ragged, like a scrap of old cotton cloth. All night long, voices interrupted my sleep with cries: "Mother, Big Brother! Help! It hurts! I'm in pain! Somebody come!"

When I got up, my uncle advised, "You should leave now while it is still cool outside." So I decided to start my search early. The streets in the Ujina district were deadly quiet and as I headed toward the Government Tax and Monopoly Bureau, I came across mountains of corpses. A foul smell assailed my nostrils.

Hiroshima was unrecognizable. I was frightened by the people I saw, wobbling around so badly burned that they barely looked human. It seemed impossible that they were still alive.

"Water... Water... Give me water...." With both arms outstretched, burnt bodies stumbled toward me in desperation. I was terrified by what I saw and wanted to run as far away as possible. On the first day of my search, survivors would approach me and politely ask, "Please give me some water.... Please let me have some water," but today, the victims were barely capable of whispering, "Water... Water..." I gave the people water to drink from my canteen, but my hands were shaking uncontrollably in fear.

Someone called out to me from behind. He had heard that giving water to people with such serious injuries would probably kill them. In spite of this, another man, whose body was completely burned on one side, cried out, "I don't care if I die. *Water*... I want some water. My throat is burning! Hurry! Hurry up. Water... Water..." His voice gradually became fainter and fainter. I wasted no time and gave the poor creature with the outstretched arms some water.

Scenes such as this recurred repeatedly. From the moment I arrived in Hiroshima, I felt as if I were suffocating. Each day was as sorrowful and torturous as the one before. There were times that I was so weary — both emotionally and physically — that I lay down in resignation alongside the dead and dying. Somehow, I mustered up the strength and courage to stand up and continue my search.

I crossed the Miyuki Bridge and was about to search for a place to rest when I heard in the distance a conversation between a child and an elderly person.

"You know, Grandpa, my eyes don't hurt so bad now," said the little girl. "But I still can't see anything. If only I could see, I'd take out all the glass from your back."

"That's enough, Masako-chan," the grandfather replied firmly. "Your fingers must hurt more than my back. The glass doesn't need to be taken out."

I walked in the direction of the sweet soft voices and within seconds I saw that the grandfather's face, hands, and back were covered in dark blood. Part of his right hand was missing. He had wrapped his other arm around his granddaughter, and the two of them were nestled close to each other.

I took a deep breath and went up to the old man, asking him if I could help in any way. He explained that he and his granddaughter had been on their way back home from a nearby field when there was a sudden flash. "I found myself pinned under a shack. I managed to crawl out and as I began searching for my granddaughter, a large iron bar fell in front of me. I tried to lift up the bar with my hand, but in the process, my five fingertips were cut off, sheared off by the searing hot bar. When this happened, I didn't think about the pain. I was more concerned about Masako. Like a madman, I searched for her everywhere. I finally heard a little voice cry out, 'My eyes hurt! My eyes hurt....'"

The old man paused for a minute as he looked helplessly at his blind granddaughter. "Masako hasn't been able to see since. With me leading her by the hand, we finally found our way back to our house. But as we were standing at the back door of our house, shards of glass from a second-story window came crashing down, and the small shattered pieces embedded themselves in my back. Despite her loss of sight, Masako tried to remove the pieces of glass. That is why her fingertips are so badly hurt," he said as he showed me his granddaughter's bloody hands.

"The poor thing, the poor thing," he continued, bent over with grief. "I wish I had died instead of being injured like this — at least then Masako wouldn't be burdened with having to care for me!"

The grandfather burst out crying. I was totally paralyzed. I did not know how to help this man and could not even find any words to comfort him. I felt useless. After a few minutes, I composed myself and took out what was left of the medicine from my bag. I told him that I did not have enough for them both, not even enough medicine to cover his entire back, so I would apply it to the worst areas.

The old man wiped his tears with the back of his left hand, and whispered, "Yes. Yes, thank you very much, but I'm already an old man. It doesn't matter what happens to me, but because Masako is still a child — what an awful thing to happen to her." He began to sob again.

I told him that I would have to remove the glass before applying the medicine.

He bowed his head, saying over and over again, "I'm very grateful. It's better than I deserve."

I carefully removed each piece of glass that I could see protruding from his skin, and gently probed his skin for more pieces as I proceeded. I finally finished, and it seemed that my tenderly stroking his skin to search for the glass and removing it made him feel somewhat better.

"Now that we have got that out of the way, I can put some medicine on for you," I told him gently. "I'm sorry — it will sting as I put it on."

The old man refused, however, to allow me to use any of the medicine on him. He looked at me with imploring eyes as he held his granddaughter with his better arm and said, "I'm much better already since you removed the glass. I beg of you, please use the medicine for Masako instead."

I nodded and turned toward Masako-chan, asking her to put out her hands, but she hid them behind her back. She started to cry in a loud voice, "Masako's fine! Masako's fine! It doesn't hurt anymore! Put medicine on Grandpa."

No matter how hard I tried, the little girl would not hold out her hands. I was struck by what a kind-hearted child she was. I felt ashamed, knowing that if I were in her place I might have gladly accepted the medicine.

But her grandfather insisted that it was he who really didn't need the medicine. Her grandpa, seeing her trying to help him rather than accepting the help she herself needed, urged her to accept the treatment. "Masako, Grandpa had all the glass taken out of his back — it's fine for now. Masako, let her put some on you now."

"Uh-uh, uh-uh, Grandpa first," she said. She would not yield. I was deeply touched by their noble hearts. I asked myself a question that had crossed my mind a lot lately: How could such a sweet, kind, and selfless child be inflicted with such pain and suffering?

I decided I had to do what I thought was best. "Well, then, let's first take care of Grandpa. If there's some medicine left over, then we'll put some on Masako-chan, OK?"

The little girl reluctantly gave her consent. The grandfather bowed his head in agreement. He said, "Well then, go ahead please," but his eyes instead implored me, "Please don't use much on me. Save it for my grandchild, my little Masako-chan."

"Are you ready for the medicine? It will hurt," I told him. "Do you think you can bear it OK?"

"Yes, yes, of course I can take it. After all," he said with a twinkle in his eye, "I'm Masako's grandpa."

I slowly and gently applied medicine to his deepest wounds. "Oh, oh, it stings," he flinched.

"Grandpa, does it hurt? Does it? Does it hurt?" Masako-chan felt her way to her Grandpa's side.

"Yes, it hurts, but it's helping me. I feel better already, Masako. Soon your Grandpa will be able to give you a piggy-back ride."

Masako giggled with happiness and embarrassment. "Grandpa, Masako's seven. If you give me a piggyback ride, everybody'll laugh! I *can* walk, after all."

"Yes, you're right," Grandpa agreed. "What was I thinking?"

When I thought I had used all I should for her grandfather, I turned to Masako. "Now it is Masako-chan's turn. Put out your hands, my dear."

Poor thing! She winced as she hesitantly and painfully opened her hands to reveal her delicate little fingers, which were horribly cut.

"Well, Masako-chan, try and be as brave as you can," I said, as I applied the Mercurochrome. Her fingers quivered as she tried her best to endure the pain.

When I used up all the medicine I had, we all felt relieved. I suggested that we celebrate with some rice balls that I had packed. But, as she had before, Masako-chan insisted that it was only her grandfather who needed my help. "Masako is fine," she said, "I'm not hungry. Please give my share to Grandpa." She explained that the day before her grandfather had given all the food he had found to Masako and had not eaten anything himself. "And so, today, I don't need anything."

I told her not to worry, that I had enough rice balls for all of us. She seemed reassured by my words and took out a homemade handkerchief from her pocket, laid it across her lap, and waited patiently for the food. The three of us sat down to eat, with Masako-chan sitting between us.

I was struck once more by Masako's pure and generous spirit. She was concerned that her grandfather might not be eating his share of the rice balls and repeatedly asked to make sure, "You *are* eating some, aren't you?" This simple act of caring made me appreciate how delicious the rice balls were and indeed made me more aware of everything I had in life — but had taken for granted up to this point.

We talked as we ate, and when I had finished eating, I explained to the old man and his granddaughter that I would have to leave soon to continue my search for my family members. Before I left, I took out all of the remaining provisions from my bag and gave them to the child: six pieces of candy, toilet paper, a note pad, and a washrag.

"Masako-chan, I'm placing your grandpa in your care," I told her.

"I understand," she replied steadily.

I took Masako-chan's hands in mine and wished her goodbye. She would not let go of my hands for the longest time. In spite of her brave words and tone it was clear she did not want me to leave. I reassured her that I would return the next day.

She replied, "Masako will be here too. Grandpa will be here tomorrow too, right?" she asked him. We all promised each other we would meet the next day.

There was not really much more I could do for them, but I still could not help but think about what would become of them and how the two could possibly survive in such conditions. It broke my heart to think of their suffering and their probable fate. Even though we had only just met, I had grown very close to them.

"Tomorrow, then," we said as we separated.

When I looked back at them, Masako-chan had linked hands with her grandpa. With a slight tilt of her head to one side, she turned and waved at me.

I decided that it would probably be a good idea to head home now and go out and look for my brother's children in the afternoon. Where were they? Were they injured like the little girl? What was going through their heads at this moment? I tried to block those thoughts out, but I was truly scared for my young niece and nephew who were out there, alone and helpless.

For what purpose, and for whose benefit, is war?

The Boy Who Went Beddy-Bye with His Mommy

Afternoon, August 8, 1945

I returned home for a few hours and was thinking about resting for the remainder of the afternoon, but I knew that would somehow be irresponsible of me. So when my uncle asked about the search, I told him that I would go out again.

I set out once more and had not walked very far when I felt a sharp pain in the sole of my left foot. A pebble had worked its way into my ripped sneaker and cut my foot. I tended to my foot and wearily resumed walking the streets, wondering where on earth I should look for my niece and nephew.

When I had traveled as far as the Sixth District, I came upon an elderly woman sitting in the middle of the road, staring absently into space. The sight of this woman triggered thoughts about my own mother, who was waiting for me to return home to the island. I not only had responsibilities to her, but also to the children I taught. Tomorrow would be the third day of absence from my knitting class. The children were probably worried about me and wondering when, if ever, I would return. My heart ached at the thought of my friends and family who were waiting for me. How I longed to go home to my island!

Feelings of guilt washed over me as I realized that I had not yet written one letter to my mother since I had arrived in Hiroshima. She must be frantic with fear. How could I have been so thoughtless? I decided there and then that regardless of how tired I was, I would write a letter to her when I got back tonight.

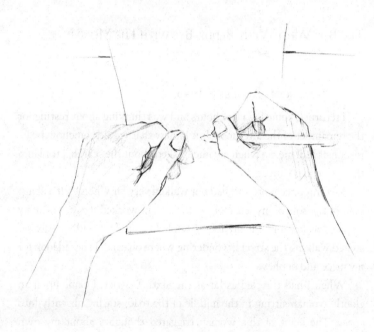

Dear Mother,

As I write, the sky is burning red, and I imagine that from our home on Osaki-shimo Island, the mountains surrounding Hiroshima must also look red. You must be lonely all by yourself. Please try to wait patiently for me, though. I know you wanted to go to Hiroshima yourself to search, but now that I am here, I can tell you that it was a good thing that I came instead. I think it would have been too hard on you. I am doing fine though, searching hard each day.

Oh, Mom, you would be sick if you saw up close what horrors have struck Hiroshima! I went to my brother's house to survey the extent of the damage. Mother, the house is so badly burned that it is hard to imagine that this was ever their house at all. When I look at the ruins, I can't remember the way their house once looked.

It is strange to think that just a few days ago, Hiroshima was intact and there was order and calm. Now, every day the situation seems to dramatically worsen. In places that yesterday didn't seem so badly affected, today corpses are piled up like mountains. It is as if I am in a totally different world. This reality is far more frightening and cruel than the stories of hell that Father used to tell me when I was a child. I try to shut my eyes as much as possible against the horror.

I have something terrible to tell you, Mother, and I don't know how. This afternoon, I saw a very young child crying amongst the smoldering ruins of my elder brother's neighborhood. "Little One, come here and I'll give you a hug. Do you want a piggyback ride? Would you like a rice ball? What a good boy."

No matter what I said, though, the child wouldn't stop crying. "Please stop crying, won't you? Hey, come over here — I'll give you a hug," I told him.

He shook his head and tried to push my hands away. He was trying to say something, but I couldn't make out the words because he was crying so hard. When I put my ear up to his mouth, it sounded like he was saying "Mommy."

"What's wrong with your Mommy?" I asked. This made him howl even louder. I looked around to see if I could spot someone who might be his mother, but there was no one. I didn't know what to do.

At a loss, I sat down for a while. Then, the boy pointed his finger and said, "I want to go beddy-bye with my Mommy."

"Where's your Mommy?" I followed the boy's finger with my eyes, and saw that he was pointing to the burnt ruins of a house and a broken piece of concrete, where a hand was visible.

I couldn't believe my eyes. I whispered, "Is that your Mommy?"

The little boy nodded his head and started crying and hiccupping again. "I want to go beddy-bye with my Mommy," he repeated.

The child just cried and cried and refused to be comforted. Mother, how could I possibly tell him that his mother was dead and would never put him to bed again? How can you explain death to an innocent little child who is crying out for his mommy? The little boy, with tears still streaming down his face, walked up to me and told me once more, pointing, "I want to go beddy-bye with my Mommy!"

I couldn't bear seeing the poor child in such agony, so I told him I would put him down with his Mommy if he would stop crying. He immediately stopped crying and looked up at me with expectant eyes. The minute those words came out of my mouth, I regretted them. How could I possibly give this boy what he wanted? Suddenly I was the one who wanted to bawl.

"Well, come on," I said, still unsure of what to do next. "I'll put you to sleep with your Mommy." He obediently took my hand. I wondered how to hold him without hurting him; he was burned beyond description. When I touched him, blood and parts of his skin stuck to my hands. I gave him a hug as gently as I could. His hands — his entire body — were swollen and red. I led the boy to the ruins where his mother's hand was visible. I tried to clean up a bit and then sat down.

"Come sit here," I told him, pointing to an open spot beside me. As soon as he sat down, I rolled up my sleeves and immediately set about digging. It took me a long time to dig, since I lacked the strength and spirit to make much headway.

After what seemed to be an eternity, I uncovered the face of a woman. I asked the boy (who had quietly moved to my side) to tell me if this was his mother. I turned the face toward the boy. He nodded. Her face wasn't in very bad shape, but the rest of her body was totally scarred and burned. From her chest protruded a bone, and many large nails were stuck into her. I turned white at the sight of her. The boy did not even flinch, but looked at her intently without blinking.

I told him to sit down behind me, and I resumed digging the hole for him to lie down next to his mother. I got in the hole myself to check whether he would have adequate space. I had no problem in fitting in the space, so I turned toward the little boy to let him know that he could come over and lie down next to his mommy.

As I turned, I found that he had been standing next to me all the time while I was digging, watching my progress carefully. My body was grimy with sweat and dirt, especially my hands and feet. I removed all of the rocks, nails, wires, and other debris, then spread out my hand towel and announced that his spot was ready. He rewarded me with a sweet smile.

"Let's have something to eat first," I suggested, "and then you can go beddy-bye with your mommy." He nodded in agreement and reached out with his pitiful, burned hands for a rice ball and some green tea. I felt a sense of relief at being able to do something concrete to help this poor orphan.

After he had finished eating, I told him, "Well then, your Big Sister is going away for a little while, so do you really want to go beddy-bye here with your Mommy?" He bobbed his head up and down in response.

My hands shaking like a leaf, I placed the boy beside his mother's body in the hole I had made. He nestled in beside her easily. The boy stretched out his hand to grasp his mother's hand. "How is it?" I asked. He looked at me and again smiled.

I told him, "It must be nice for you, Little One. I'd like to hold hands with *my* Mommy and go beddy-bye too." He smiled once more. I slipped my hand in around his body to make sure there was no debris left that might hurt him. "Will you be OK? Can you stretch your legs out? Can you lay up against your Mommy, Little One?" Uncomfortable with his being in such a place, I kept asking him, "Do you hurt anywhere? Don't your arms and legs hurt?"

He soon began to breathe more easily, his eyes slowly closing. I don't know whether he was incredibly tired or felt comforted by being close to his mother, but as he slept, his head nestled against her shoulder. I felt relieved to see the boy sleeping peacefully next to her. I sat there for a while, mesmerized, not able to take my eyes off them.

However, the glare of the afternoon sun was shining on the boy's face. That won't do, I thought. I reluctantly lifted him out of the hole. Using the charred remains of a board and a galvanized iron sheet I found nearby, I tried to construct a sort of awning for him.

Since I had woken him up, I asked if I could give him a hug first before I put him back with his Mommy. He reached out to grab hold of me and climbed into my lap. He pressed his face into my chest and wrapped his little arms around my waist. I caressed his face as I held him. Mother, I can't remember the last time I felt so happy, seeing the contentment radiating from his face.

I asked him how old he was, and with his face still pressed to me, he stuck out three fingers. I treated the terrible wounds on each of his fingers. His poor ears were even more horribly hurt — one of them seemed about to fall

off. I then put medicine on his ears, and then bandaged
his head to help protect the ears and the other wounds.

After a while, I reluctantly looked at my watch. Four
hours had passed since I had arrived here. I thought to
myself that even though I had not yet managed to find
my niece and nephew, at least I had succeeded in making
him happier. I soon started to worry, though, about what
would happen when the boy woke up and realized his
mother could no longer respond to his needs. I thought
that by the time I returned to him I might be more easily

able to convince him to leave his mother and go home with me to let me take care of him.

So, once more, I asked him, "Little One, do you want to go beddy-bye with your Mommy? Can you get up?" I helped him get up from my lap, but by now he was shaky and quickly leaned on me for support. He looked so tired. I asked if he was OK, but he just stared at me and didn't reply.

I then gently lifted him into my arms and put him in the hole. After checking to see if he was OK, I placed a hand towel under the boy's head and placed his mother's hand, which was now cold, in his. The child's face was filled with serenity and a calm happiness. I shivered at the prospect of him waking up to this awful reality. I couldn't help but burst into tears. You poor thing, you poor thing, I thought to myself. You don't understand that your mother is dead! My heart filled with sorrow and anger as I thought of the little boy growing up without his mother.

Mother, how can such a thing be allowed to happen? Since I've arrived in Hiroshima, I have been struggling with overwhelming feelings of anger and frustration, pain and sadness. I have seen up close how painful, how sorrowful, how cruel war is — I have seen it by touching it with my hands, hearing the tortured cries of children, smelling the terror and carnage. Every night I cry myself to sleep until there are no more tears.

As I braced myself to leave the boy and his poor mother in search of my elder brother's children, I looked at him once more. He opened his eyes for a few moments and looked into my face, and then quietly closed his eyes. I caressed his forehead one last time and gently touched his cheek. I prayed with all my heart and soul that somehow this child would get well.

However, when I touched his forehead, it seemed as though he had a fever. It worried me, so I took him out of the hole once again. His body was growing limp. I asked yet another time whether he would like to go beddy-bye with his Mommy. Again, he nodded his head up and down, so I put him back next to his mother.

"Here, hold your mommy's hand," I whispered, and he held on to it tightly. "You close your eyes, Little One." I thought that the medicine would begin to work while he slept and so he would feel a little better when he woke. I stood up and began to walk away, but from time to time, I turned around and looked back.

I lost track of time as I walked the city, calling out the names of my elder brother's children. My feet started to give way underneath me. No longer able to continue, I squatted down in exhaustion. A voice right near my feet startled me, pleading, "Water... Water... Water..." Off to my side was what I had assumed was a corpse — only the skeleton remained, dry and scorched like a dead tree. I suddenly felt very cold and started to shiver in fear.

Mother, you have no idea how horrible it is! Where can I go to escape such sickening scenes? I do take comfort, though, that I came instead of you.

I continued searching for a while longer, but I soon began to stagger with exhaustion, so I decided to return to the boy to see how he was. I knelt down next to him, rested my head on his back, and whispered into his ear that I had returned.

But he did not respond to my words. His body was completely still and he had no pulse. I realized that the child was dead, still holding his mommy's hand. I shrieked in despair. "Ah... Ah... I've done such an awful thing! What did I do? Little One, Little One, it's your Big Sister!"

I could see only half of the boy's face. The scraps of board and sheet iron that I had placed together to protect this three-year-old boy from the sun had ended up falling on his face and killing him. As I realized what I had done, I cried out for my own mother....

I then cried out to the little boy for forgiveness. "Little One, I'm sorry! I am so sorry!" Desperately, I removed the debris that had fallen on his now disfigured face. "*I killed him!* It was I who killed this boy! I made this hole, and I put him in it and left him!" I screamed, shouting out my guilt to whoever could hear me.

I wanted to jump out of my skin and escape from myself. I had become a monster. I yelled out, "I should have taken him to my house *when I first saw him*, no matter how much he cried. I should have known better. He was just a little child. I should have made the decision for him. Then this wouldn't have happened. I didn't stop to think that this might happen. Forgive me, Little One. No matter what I say now, you won't come back to life. Oh, what an idiot I am! I thought I was helping you, but I ended up killing you! I'm a horrible, horrible person!"

Mother, what should I have done? Please tell me! If it had been you, what would you have done? There are no excuses for what happened. I don't know what came over me.

Gently, I lifted up the boy and cradled him in my arms. "How it must have hurt you. Please forgive your Big Sister, Little One. I am so sorry." Looking at his injured face, I hugged the boy tightly and cried uncontrollably.

I did not know what to do with the child's body. I finally decided to return him to his mother's side; he would certainly be happiest there. I placed him back in the hole with his hand holding his mother's, and tied their hands together with a ribbon.

I asked the boy's mother for forgiveness, again and again. But even so, I knew that no matter how much I apologized, no matter how much I cried, he wouldn't come back to life. On some scratch paper I wrote, "Please don't separate this mother and child. I beg you." I placed the note over their hands and set a pebble on it. I staggered back to my Uncle's home, a mere shadow of myself.

As soon as I got home tonight, I ran up to my room. I couldn't face seeing anyone.

God, what can I do to get your forgiveness? God, *please* forgive me. I don't care what happens to me — if only you could forgive me. *How* did I end up doing something so *cruel*?

Mother, I hope that you too can forgive me. At the time, I couldn't think of anything else to do. What an idiot I am. I killed a child, and because of this, I no longer know who I am. My heart is torn with fear. I am so sorry, but my remorse accomplishes nothing. I ask myself again and again what I should have done instead.

I am aching to go home now. My whole body is stiff and sore, and my heart has been torn to shreds. Mother, I need you to stroke my weary head and tell me that everything is going to be all right. I am filled with such sorrow this evening that I can't even cry.

Will the little boy and his mommy in Heaven understand that I didn't mean to harm him? Do they know how truly sorry I am? If only I had died instead... So many innocent lives have been lost, yet I am still living. What justice is there in that? What happened today will always be emblazoned in my memory. I will never stop praying to God for forgiveness, and the memory of this boy will remain with me. The anguish and heartbreak I feel for him is even stronger than the memory of my dead father and younger brother Masao.

I cannot afford to allow my misery to overcome me. I still have to continue searching for your grandchildren. I never thought I'd be away from home this long. No matter how hard I search for your grandchildren, I can't find them. I probably never will. No — I can't think that way, can I? I *will* bring them home at any cost. By the time this letter reaches you, I may have already found them.

Mother, you'll probably be shocked when you read this letter. I can almost see you leaning out of our second-story window, the memories still fresh in your mind of my brothers who went off to war. But now, because I've told you everything, my heart is a little lighter. I can breathe again and am no longer suffocated with guilt. I am determined to do all I can to find my niece and nephew, and to help the other children I come across. Please try not to worry too much. I have faith that I'll bring them home.

Mother, war has always inflicted pain upon those who are gentle, pure, and innocent, leaving them scarred. I want to cry out for the boy that I killed, "Please stop making war — we've had enough!" Mother, why is it still forbidden to speak out against war? I can't believe we have to keep quiet. If I am in such pain having killed one child, I cannot imagine how tortured those people must be who have taken countless lives!

Can we afford to shrug our shoulders and say, "This is war, and so it can't be helped"? No. I believe that the time will come when we *will* be able to speak out loud and clear against war, certainly and without fail. When that time comes, I will cry out on behalf of this little boy, and in defense of *all* the children who are victims of war:

Enough is enough! Never again! *Certainly and without fail.*

Yours,

Sadako

My Mother Wears Glasses Too

August 9, 1945

Since my arrival in Hiroshima, I have struggled each morning to get out of bed and prepare myself physically and mentally for the day's search, and today was no exception. I got dressed hurriedly, even though I was so weak and tired. Surely, it would make more sense for me to rest and conserve my energy for the following day.

My uncle was sympathetic but he nonetheless encouraged me to persist in the search for my niece and nephew. Perhaps I had seen so much horror by now that in a way I have become accustomed to it. At least I no longer felt like throwing up as often as I had. I decided that I would head out yet again but perhaps return early and rest a bit if I had no luck.

With a heavy heart I rushed through breakfast and set out with heavy steps. I had only been walking for about an hour, but it felt as if I had been walking for days. I grew more and more fatigued with each step. I lost my sense of balance and stumbled over some debris, and I stepped on an old nail that was protruding from a wooden board. The pain was excruciating. As I lifted my right foot, the board came up with it. I took a deep breath, closed my eyes, and pulled the nail out of my foot, which was now bleeding steadily. It hurt so much I had to sit down. I tried to stretch my legs out, and though I am petite, the ground was too covered in corpses and debris for me to find enough space to do so. There was more open space near the cistern of water reserved for fighting fires, so I hobbled over there to rest. But instead of finding water inside the cistern, I was sickened to find corpses piled one on top of each other. Nauseated, I hopped to a spot slightly farther away and found a place where I could sit and rest.

The throbbing sensation was no longer solely limited to my foot; my head was now pounding and dizziness overcame me. I examined my foot and applied some medicine to it. My wound was extremely deep. I would probably not be able to continue my search for several hours. I was debating whether to head back home to rest when I felt a light tap on my shoulder from behind. Distracted, I realized that the weight of a little hand on my shoulder had moved to rest gently on my throat. I slowly turned my head and found that a swollen and burned, ravaged hand, with the skin hanging off it, was gently resting on my shoulder. The gentle hand was that of a little boy who could not have been more than four years old. The boy's short pants revealed his legs, so badly burned that you couldn't bear to look at them.

The little boy did not cry or speak. He just stood there and stared at me intensely. With great effort I stood up and tested to see if I could walk with my injured foot. When I did, he came to stand even closer to me. Without saying a word, he grabbed my little finger very tightly.

The way that he held onto my finger supported me and helped me to walk slowly, a few steps at a time. Because of my injured foot, the child's small footsteps suited me just fine. We did not say anything to each other, but I could not help but feel connected to this little boy as we walked side by side in harmony. When the child stopped to rest, so did I. After a while, though, the boy began to show signs of being tired, so I got down on my hands and knees and let him climb on my back. He clung tightly to me and I gave him a piggyback ride.

I didn't know where I was or how I had come to the place where I found myself, but we had come to a place more terrible than any other, near the center of the explosion. This place, a scar that must have been made by the fingernail of the devil himself — marred by utmost evil — was more horrific than any of the other areas I had seen. Before me was a wasteland, barren but for the dead bodies that filled virtually every inch of the ground. I wanted to scream but the only sound that escaped my mouth was a deep moan.

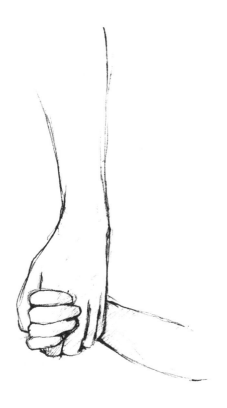

Behind me, a soldier was pouring fuel oil over a pile of dead bodies and was setting them alight. My nostrils were filled with a sickening stench as body parts were set on fire. I heard a sound too ghastly for words. As charred corpses burned and burst open, the internal organs exploded, boiling on the galvanized iron sheets on which they lay. Tearing my attention away from that horrific sight, I saw right in front of me an older child, who perhaps a few days ago had been in middle school but who now was collapsed on the ground, covered in blood. Before I could act, an old person tripped and fell on him, trembled two or three times in something like a convulsive fit, and then ceased to move. It was complete and utter hell on earth.

I was filled with intense wrath and unbounded grief. I could not even take two steps without standing on yet another corpse. Amidst the mass of corpses, I saw a young girl walking with skin hanging from her face, neck, and hands. A boy stood before a mountain of corpses, staring at it as if his spirit had left his body. I tried to avert my gaze from him and the dead bodies, but my eyes would not cooperate as they took in the sight of young boys and girls with eyeballs dangling from their sockets. Living and dead, who could distinguish them?

My thoughts were interrupted when I felt something tug at my *mompé*. I looked down to find a woman crying at my feet, "Mother, help me, Mother..." She cried, "Please give me some water. Water. My throat is burning!" When I gave her some, she clasped her hands together two or three times, saying, "Thank you," but then her eyes quietly closed.

I walked around in circles, carrying the child on my back. I stooped down low as I walked, ashamed to be alive and well when so many around me were dead or severely injured. As we approached the river, I grew dizzy. A sea of bodies too numerous to count were floating in the water, rising and falling with the waves. Some bodies were bloated to twice their normal size, the skin purple. I could not take it anymore. A soul can only absorb so much devastation before it shuts down in protest. I sat down on the ground and curled up into a ball, withdrawing into myself.

I even forgot about the little boy I had been carrying on my back. Some time later, when I started to regain awareness, I discovered that the child was gone. I looked for him in every direction, but I could not see him. Who was that child who had disappeared from my life as quietly and quickly as he had entered it?

I was perspiring heavily by this point. Just looking at the burnt bodies made me feel like my skin was on fire. I found myself succumbing to the urge to cool myself, to put water on my arms, legs, and head, so I walked back down to the river. But there was no relief to be found from such a river of death. In front of me, I saw some young students lying dead in the water with what appeared to be their teacher. They must not have been able to endure the heat of their burns, and so they had died as they ventured into the fearsome river to try to cool their skin. Now they moved with the current of the river, along with the corpses of thousands.

The scene reminded me of a book that my older brother had read to me when I was young. The book depicted a fearful hell that would be the end of the earth, and I felt as if I were now seeing that hell. I had always assumed that if such a cataclysm were to take place, it would be the result of something I thought would be more significant and powerful than a war.

I stood in the center of that fearful hell in a daze — my vision blurred. From my trance, I felt a warm little hand take firm hold of mine and pull me out. I looked down to see that the little boy had returned to my side. For my part, I had no energy to speak so I was relieved that the boy was still silent. We continued walking as if we had never been separated, two hands holding each other in comfort and support.

After a while, though, the boy stopped. He was too tired to continue walking, so once again, I got down on my hands and knees and told him to climb on my back, but this time he hesitated. I asked him if he was hungry or wanted some tea, but as usual, he did not respond. So, I picked him up and staggered on my way.

Each step that I took was difficult and agonizing. I told myself that unless I stop now, I will collapse — and then what state would I be in to search for my niece and nephew? But I forced myself to keep walking. I could not give up.

I noticed that there were boards propped up against the debris at the sides of the streets. People had written messages on these boards to missing family members. I put down the little boy and used one of the scraps of boards to write a message:

> Fuyo-chan and Yukiaki-chan,
> We're waiting at your uncle's house in Ujina.
> Sadako

I propped it up with the others. I closed my eyes and prayed they would come across it.

As I stood there deep in thought, an old man on the ground tugged at my ankle. He pointed desperately to the identification tags on his chest. When I knelt down to read the name on the tag, he summoned his remaining strength and whispered, "Please, write on the board over there that I am dead, so that my children and grandchildren will see it when they come to look for me. Please, I beg of you."

I responded, "I could not possibly do that. Please try to be strong. Maybe everything will be all right." He begged me again and again to write the message. I looked at this poor man and realized what he must have been feeling. I understood his desire to let his family know that there was no need to continue searching for him. So I made sure once again that he really wanted me to write that he had died, and then complied with his wishes and wrote the message for him. When I finished, he inhaled deeply and a peaceful expression grew upon his face.

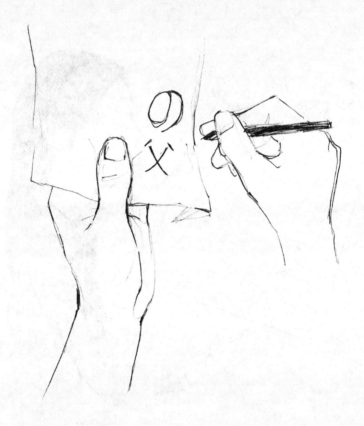

While I was busy with the old man, the little boy once again disappeared, but a few minutes later he emerged from the back of a nearby burnt-down building and we started walking again. Curiosity finally overcame me and I asked the little boy his name and age, but no matter what I asked, he would not say anything. But when I asked him, "Do you want to come home with me?" he quickly grabbed hold of my *mompé*. We continued walking for some time, but he grew weary once more and I carried him on my back until we reached my uncle's house.

By the time we arrived home, evening had come with a strangely beautiful sunset. The child had fallen asleep on my back. I tried to gently lay him down on my bed but he immediately woke up. My uncle offered him some sugar water, and he drank it in one gulp and stuck out his cup for more.

"It must be good," my uncle said as he refilled his glass. "You seem to be in good spirits." My uncle turned to me and winked. "You did a good thing, Sadako, bringing him here." And as if reading my mind, he continued, "Don't worry, he'll be just fine."

Once the little boy had finished drinking, I tried to take off his jacket to clean him up. At first he flinched and pulled away, but eventually he acquiesced and let me take off his jacket. I then removed the boy's torn shirt and came to understand why he had resisted. I was appalled to see the wound he had borne under his clothes. In the middle of his back, about four inches of his flesh had been scooped out and the wound had turned dark purple.

I got the supplies I needed and treated him. My uncle sat down next to the boy and asked me to tell him how I had found him. I described the day's events and told him that even though the boy had to be in a great deal of pain, he had not uttered a sound. Then the boy stuck out his cup again for more sugar water. You really can't speak, I thought to myself. Poor thing.

"My mommy wears 'em too." I nearly jumped out of my skin when I heard the boy say that to my uncle.

I couldn't believe my ears. Wanting to make sure that I was not just imagining that he had spoken, I asked if he could say that again. But this time he did not open his mouth.

My uncle explained, "He said that his mother wears glasses too. Now that he is in our house, he feels safer and more secure. He saw my glasses and it reminded him of his mother. I'm sure that he was thinking of his mother all along. The poor boy is suffering from such trauma that he can't even cry, let alone speak." I saw that my uncle must be right, but I couldn't help but try to get him to talk to me again.

Before long, the little boy began to rub his eyes. "Ahhh, you're tired, aren't you," I said. "Come take a nap with your Big Sister."

I carefully placed him on his side because of the wound in his back. I lay down next to him and held him in my arms. He wrapped his arm around my neck. The little boy looked into my eyes for the longest time. But soon exhaustion overcame him and several minutes later he was fast asleep in my arms, breathing peacefully.

I held this sleeping child protectively in my arms, gazing at his sweet face, relieved that he was no longer in pain. I wondered who his parents were and what had happened to them. Before long, I too became tired and allowed myself to drift off.

When I woke up, I was unsure how long I had been sleeping. Suddenly remembering the little boy in my arms, I lightly touched his cheek and was shocked to find his body had grown cold. Nestled in my arms, he had already gone to a place where I could not reach him.

My uncle hurried in when he heard me cry out, and we gazed together at the little boy in my arms. "His face is the face of peace," my uncle said.

In the midst of this devastating war, this child, whose name I did not know, had captured my heart. He had sustained horrific wounds and had been robbed of his mother who was most precious to him, yet he did not utter a single word of complaint, hatred, pain, or sadness.

Matthew 18:3 teaches us, "You must become like a little child." My experience with this little boy reinforced the truth of those words. Although we must speak out in the strongest terms against war, so that such cruelty will never happen again, at the same time we should never forget that hatred is destructive. Even as I publish this for the first time [referring to the original Japanese edition] some 34 years after the war, there are many older people in Japan who still strongly hate America. However, this little boy taught me that hate is futile and that we should channel our energy instead toward loving people and praying to God to help us overcome all the challenges and ordeals we face.

When will the war end? How long will it continue?

Today, yet again, I was unable to save a child. His glowing eyes illuminated my heart. I say a prayer and entrust his spirit to God.

Best Friends Forever

Morning, August 10, 1945

Every morning, as I left the house to begin the search, I prayed that today would be the day that I would come home with my elder brother's children.

While it was still early morning, the ground was not yet hot and I was able to walk comfortably. At times, I was even able to run, but the weight of the canteen and first-aid bag as well as other supplies on my back chafed against my shoulders and slowed me down. Now and then, I would ease the pain by lifting the straps off my shoulder with my hands.

One day blurred into another and I could no longer recognize certain areas and parts of the city, even those that I had already visited. My sense of time was also off kilter. Minutes turned into hours, which turned into days. I had no idea how many days I had been searching or how many hours I had been walking.

"Fuyoko-chan! Yuki-chan!" I cried out time and again. I racked my brain to think of places where they could possibly be and it struck me that I had not yet searched their school playground. For all I knew, they may have found refuge there, I thought with optimism in my heart. My heart sank immediately, though, when I saw they were not to be

found there, either. The playground was filled with parents and grandparents, many of them suffering from serious burns themselves, who
also harbored hopes of finding their young ones here. Parents called out
the names of their children repeatedly, their high-pitched cries revealing their desperation. When all they heard in response was the echo
of their own voices, they fell to the ground in despair. Seconds later,
though, they would get back up and call out their children's names,
refusing to give up hope.

I was about to leave the playground when I saw two middle school students hobbling toward me. Their burns were so grotesque that I thoughtlessly covered my eyes with my hands. It was almost impossible to make out any of their facial features. The two supported each other as they walked. They constantly fell and got back up, leading each other by the hand. I ran up to them, gently hugged them, and urged them not to walk any further. I hurriedly cleared an area around them. One of the boys seemed to be in much worse shape than his friend, and I was worried that he would die any moment. Too weak to speak, he put out his hands asking for water.

His friend argued with him. "No! Hiroshi-kun, I know that you are desperate for water. I want it too, but remember what the soldier said — the explosion may have been a poison bomb and could have poisoned our water. If you drink any, you will die. Please, hang in there a little bit more, please, for me?"

Hiroshi-kun begged, "I need to drink. My throat is burning!" He coughed and cleared his throat. "I don't care about dying. I just want some water. Please! One mouthful is all I want. Please let me have some." He reached toward me.

I was glad I was able to give him the water he wanted so badly. I lowered the canteen to his mouth, but his friend glared at me and pushed the canteen away. "What's wrong with you?" he yelled angrily. "If you let him drink water, he'll die!" I wished I knew the right thing to do. I thought, if I give a drink of water to this boy and his friend is right, he will probably die. But if I don't, the boy will be in agonizing pain and will die soon anyway. Surely, it was better to grant this poor boy his wish? I decided I could not deny the boy the water that he so badly craved. Hiroshi-kun's pleas for water became more and more desperate, but his voice gradually grew weaker.

I turned to Hiroshi-kun's friend and whispered into his ear. "I'm afraid there's not much hope for Hiroshi-kun. He is going to die whether he drinks water or not, so why don't we at least do this for him? OK?"

He thought about what I said and replied firmly, "No, it isn't right. We promised each other that we would stick together, even in death. If one of us has to die, the other should too. I won't have it that Hiroshi-kun dies and I am left behind."

The boy turned back to his friend and begged him once more to reconsider. "Hiroshi-kun, *I want water too*! I feel like there's a fire burning in the pit of my stomach. I beg you, hang in there, please! Please? I can't lose you now." Crying uncontrollably, he held on tight to Hiroshi-kun's hand.

Hiroshi-kun was no longer able to speak. He could now only reach toward me. Anger stirred inside me at Hiroshi-kun's friend. I lashed out at him without thinking, "You call yourself a friend? If I were in your situation, at a time like this, I would let him drink no matter how I felt. The boy is dying and he wants water so much. How can you deny him that?"

Hiroshi-kun's friend got very quiet and turned toward me with the air of having made a decision. "OK, then, please give him some, but leave some for me to drink."

The two boys were in such a wretched state that my heart broke into tiny little pieces. Their burns were so terrible you could not be sure where their eyes or mouths were. I lifted the canteen of water to Hiroshi-kun's mouth and whispered into his ear, "Do you want some water now? Go ahead and drink." Hiroshi-kun opened his eyes slightly and looked at me.

I was about to pour a small amount of water into his mouth when his friend interjected, "I'll give it to him. Please let me do it." He took the cup from my hand. "There, there, Hiroshi. Here is some water. Drink as much as you want." Hiroshi drank small amounts of water at a time, taking rests between mouthfuls. The drink seemed to have given him some relief.

However, Hiroshi-kun drank only some of the water he was offered, and pushed the cup back toward the other boy. "Now it's *your* turn. Have the rest of it. I saved you half." In a small voice, he added, "Half. There's half of it," and quietly closed his eyes again.

"Hiroshi-kun, don't worry, I'm drinking half of it too." The boy sobbed loudly and pitifully. "You and I will share everything to the very end. Hiroshi-kun, don't die! Hiroshi-kun, Hiroshi-kun, we promised each other that we would always be together, the two of us, no matter what. I don't want to be left alive without you. Hiroshi-kun, you can't die!" He hugged Hiroshi-kun tightly and buried his charred face in the chest of his bosom friend. "Why didn't you listen to me? I begged you not to drink water."

I asked Hiroshi-kun's friend for forgiveness. He turned toward me and sobbed loudly in resignation, "No, it was better to let him drink."

I held both boys in my arms and lost myself in my tears, unable to do anything but hold Hiroshi-kun and his friend as he cried out in grief and pain. When there were no more tears left to cry, he began talking to me about Hiroshi-kun. I think it gave him comfort to speak to me about him.

"Hiroshi-kun's father was a soldier and was killed early on in the war. When Hiroshi-kun was in fourth grade, his mother died from malnutrition. We were next-door neighbors, so when he was left an orphan he came to live with us. We would share everything half and half; it didn't matter whether it was our lunchbox, a potato, or a tiny pickled plum. My mother loved Hiroshi-kun as much as she loved me. Everything between us was equal."

His lip trembled as he recalled all they had gone through together. At some point during the conversation, the realization hit him that Hiroshi-kun was gone. "I am alone now. What am I going to do?"

I could find no words to comfort this poor boy. Nothing I could say would change the fact that his friend, his brother, was gone forever. And for what? *Horrible war!* If Hiroshi's father had not died in the army... If his mother had had food... If we had not made war... such a beautiful friendship, like ripples in a pond, would have formed a much bigger circle of friendship and helped to build peace. These boys didn't deserve this fate.

My thoughts traveled back to my niece and nephew who were still out there somewhere, alone. I imagined the two of them crying, "Water, water," with no one to help them. I felt it was time to leave.

I gazed at the boy who was still holding Hiroshi-kun as if his life depended on it. I gently touched his head and told him that I had to leave. I struggled to find the appropriate words to say to him, but eventually told him, "Be brave and keep your chin up. You're almost a man, after all."

"Please give me water too," the boy said. "I want to drink some water."

I had been hoping that he would not ask me again for the water. And yet, I thought that the water might comfort him so he could more easily deal with his grief.

"Hiroshi-kun ended up dying. Are you sure you want water?" He opened his mouth in response. My hands trembled as I poured water into his mouth. "You two were very lucky to have such good friends in each other. Friends are very important."

"Yes, but he's dead now," he said after he drank the remaining half cup of water. "It's all over." I wrapped my arms around them both and tried to suppress my own tears for the boy's sake, praying in my heart that these two best friends would be reunited in Heaven.

"Well, it's time for me to go," I said, as always feeling that I wanted to stay forever but that I had to keep on searching. Finally, I realized he could no longer hear me, but had left to join his friend. Their lives were over before they had a chance to begin. I started to walk away, but I quickly turned around. Tearing a leaf out of my notebook, I wrote, "Please! *Do not* separate these two!"

I placed the note on top of Hiroshi-kun's body and placed a stone on top of it. There was nothing more to be done.

Insanity and Greed

Afternoon, August 10, 1945

I had no choice but to keep on going. My heart ached with misery and sadness at the thought of the two boys I had just left behind. Could I have done anything different?

I continued walking, mechanically, still searching for my niece and nephew. I stood on the riverbank and yelled out their names — maybe they were among the tortured souls trying still to find relief in the water. I continued calling out their names until I was hoarse. Even though I knew deep down that the chances of finding them here were small, I could not suppress the fresh wave of disappointment that washed over me. How could I possibly find my niece and nephew among so many tens of thousands of corpses? Exhausted and sore, I squatted down to rest by the river.

I felt a slight breeze from behind me, which was refreshing, but the sense of relief was short-lived as I inhaled the putrid smell of burning bodies. Even to this day, this nauseating smell accompanies me wherever I go. I buried my head between my knees and closed my eyes. What was the point of continuing the search? I was deluding myself and my family with false hopes that I would bring back the children. All of a sudden, I felt a delicate tap on my shoulder.

"Ah, I'm so tired," a female voice said in a strangely cheerful way.

After just a couple of days of searching, I could no longer look at someone without being terrified of what I might see. But her voice seemed almost normal, so I looked up at her face, but then immediately gasped in horror as my eyes took in the horrible apparition this woman had become. There was no way a person could mentally prepare for that kind of sight. The woman's skin was dangling off her face, and purplish-red flesh was visible where the skin once covered it. I shuddered involuntarily. I immediately lowered my eyes, but not quickly enough. My whole body tightened and wanted to escape.

The woman was virtually naked; only a few burnt remnants of what she had been wearing remained. The drawstring around her waist and the elastic around her ankles from her *mompé* were all that remained of the clothing she must have been wearing when the bomb fell. Her injuries had not been cared for in any way, and her flesh had been gouged out in several places. I felt sick to my stomach and had to try to stop myself from throwing up.

I couldn't even bear being so close to the woman. I had to leave right away. But as I stood up, the woman grabbed hold of my wrist. I wanted to scream but no sound left my mouth. Too afraid to run away and unable to free myself, I gathered enough courage to sit down beside her. I recoiled as the woman sat right beside me and placed her hand on my shoulder. She began to mutter to herself. I could not make out what she was saying. My only thought at that time was how to get away from her as quickly as possible.

The woman kept on talking, seemingly oblivious to my frantic state. She began to ask me questions and when I didn't respond, she clasped my hand once more. "Did you get any rations of rice? Hey, if you don't go quickly, your group leader will give you a hard time. It won't do to forget your ration book." She continued to babble on, jumping from subject to subject, complaining about the difficulty of getting precious goods and the difficulties of other wartime shortages.

My heart beat rapidly as I realized that the woman was mad. Terrified, I knew I had to get away from her. I pulled my hand away and said loudly, "I'll go and get my rice-ration book and come back. Thank you for telling me." But before I could stand up to leave, she grabbed my hand once more. Her grip was surprisingly powerful. The flesh had been ripped off leaving little but the bones behind. I wouldn't have dreamed that such a hand could be so strong.

As the squishy wet pulp that still clung to her bones touched my hand, I again became sick to my stomach. I shrieked hysterically, "Let go! I have to get my rice!" I started to whimper in terror. The woman looked at me quizzically and considered my words for a second, but her hand remained on top of mine. I don't know what was going through her head, but after a few minutes she let go of my hand. Adrenalin surged through my body and I started to run. As I looked back at her, I saw her reach out both arms to me. Wailing in a loud, unintelligible voice, she came after me. I ran so fast that my feet did not feel the ground. This time, I did not look back and only stopped to catch my breath when it was clear that she was out of sight.

I looked around me — I don't know how, but it seemed that I had ended up back in the Senda District, near my elder brother's house. The signboard that I had left there with a message for my niece and nephew was no longer there. There were, however, even more corpses. I put up a new signboard, but was losing hope that they would be found.

I managed to find an open space where I could rest, and I took out my canteen of water. From a distance, I saw two soldiers turning over the strewn bodies one by one, just as I had done in my first few days of searching. At first glance, it looked as if they too were searching for someone. As they came closer, though, I could see their hands at work, swiftly removing wristwatches, fountain pens, and other merely material belongings from the burnt bodies. The soldiers' pockets were bulging, with watch chains dangling out.

I was speechless. The soldiers must have sensed my presence because they abruptly stopped what they were doing and turned toward me. I glared at them and before I could say a word, they were gone. I was in complete shock. Maybe I was totally naïve, but I could not comprehend how these two soldiers could be so desensitized to the horrors around them, and so inhuman, that they could occupy themselves with stealing from the breasts of the dead. My heart boiled over with hatred and fury. I suddenly felt very cold and very alone. I no longer recognized the world. What had happened to humanity?

My thoughts were interrupted when an old woman covered in blood tugged at my *mompé*. Facing me with her hands clasped together, the woman begged, "Please let me drink some water. Even a little would be good. Please give some to me."

By now, I was all too familiar with this request and did not hesitate to take the canteen out of my bag. I laid the woman on the ground and gave her some water. There was no longer any doubt in my mind — even if it meant certain and immediate death, I would do it if it would bring relief to these people. The woman's body grew limp within min-utes. I took one final look at her before I got up. Yet another life had been extinguished.

I didn't see how I could find the strength to remain among people so badly hurt any more. I stole back to my uncle's, overwhelmed with sadness and wanting to hide from all I had seen. I ran, though I was in no shape to even walk, my water gone, all used up.

What Purpose Do Children Serve?

August 11, 1945

When I was a child going to school in Hiroshima City, I used to cross a bridge every day. The best part of the 50-minute walk to school was this bridge. I would hop and skip across it, counting my steps as I went. Now, the bridge was unrecognizable. One third of it was covered with mountains of corpses. It was a completely different place than the one I fondly remembered.

Averting my eyes as I walked, I crossed the bridge and made my way once more to the ruins of my brother's house, hoping to find my niece and nephew there. Yesterday, the area near my brother's house was cleared of most of the corpses, but today many more had taken their place. I sat down on a pile of concrete at the front of the house and pondered where I should start to look next. Since I had started my search, I was constantly battling feelings of nausea and queasiness. On the ground by my feet was the burnt corpse of a child who could not have been older than two years old. Her body resembled a large piece of whale meat that had spoiled.

The poor thing had died such a merciless death. I closed my eyes to calm my heart, rubbing my aching feet.

When I opened my eyes a few minutes later, though, I was shocked to see that the lump of flesh had stirred. Was she alive? How could that be? I knelt down by her side and looked directly into her face. Her burns were so horrific that you could not tell where her nose and mouth were. The fact that she had moved was nothing short of a marvel. In her right hand, the little one was holding onto an empty, broken cream bottle as though it were a favorite toy.

The bottle was cutting into the joint of her thumb. I attempted to remove it from her hand, but my own hands were shaking so badly that I was unsuccessful. Next to the child lay her mother's dead body. The mother had tied herself to the child's left hand with the drawstring of her *mompé*. I imagined that the mother must have done this shortly before she died, not wanting her daughter to wander off and get lost. She must have also realized that with no one else to care for her child, her daughter would die soon as well. At the very least, she did not want them to be separated from each other, even in death. As her mother must have hoped, her presence seemed to reassure her tiny daughter.

I put some bites of a rice ball in the child's mouth, a little at a time. After watching her eat a little, I gave her some green tea. I did not know what else I could do for this little girl. I certainly could not take her with me, but the thought of leaving her there to die was too awful to imagine. In the end, after wrestling with my heart, I came to the realization that I had no choice but to leave this girl. I laid her down close to her mother, and, with an aching heart, continued my search.

With a heavy heart, I started walking with no idea of where I was going. My feet seemed to have a will of their own and led me, for the second time in two days, in the direction of the river. Before I knew it, I was back at the river of hell, which was brimming over with corpses. I could not sustain my weight or the weight of the horrors in front of me, so I squatted down. I decided that I might as well head home.

On my way, I passed the Japanese Red Cross station where I saw an interminable line of wounded waiting outside. The thought entered my head that maybe my brother's children were amongst them. But I saw no sign of them as I walked up and down. I was about to leave when an elderly woman with a sleeping baby in her arms stepped in front of me.

"For mercy's sake... This child, somehow... I entreat you!" she pleaded, quickly handing the baby over to me. The child was in my arms
before I knew what was happening. Before I could take another breath,
the old woman sat down and died, having fulfilled her mission of finding someone to care for the baby.

I felt as though I was in a dream.

The baby was naked and her body was badly burned. Still in shock, holding this little child, I ran to the front of the line, to the relief squad.

"Could anyone please give this child milk?" I asked desperately. "If there's anything we can give this baby to drink... Anything would do. I beg of you.... Won't somebody help? *Please* give the child something quickly! Anything!"

Was I invisible? The expressions on the workers' faces remained blank, as if they had not heard my plea at all. I pleaded desperately to one relief worker who was just standing there. "I beg you. Please, if you have anything to put in the child's mouth, some milk or sugar or something... Anything is fine.... Please, give it to this baby!"

The relief worker turned to me and glared at me contemptuously. "Why are you asking me for help? There is nothing anyone can do for the child. How do you expect the baby to be able to survive without its parents? You must be crazy." He paused for a moment and pointed to the long line of casualties. "Look around you! Don't you think I'm busy enough with the adults? Don't waste any more of my time! This child is probably going to die, and even if it doesn't, what purpose does it serve in keeping a child like this alive? You're a nuisance. Get lost! Adults are more important than *that*," pointing to the child.

I was seething with rage and was not going to let him have the final word. "Do you mean to say that you think this child *deserves* to die? How would you feel if this were *your* child? Would you still say that there is no point keeping her alive? Wouldn't you be running around like crazy doing whatever you could to help her?" My heart was beating rapidly and the blood rose to my cheeks. "This child *is* alive and it is *our* responsibility to care for her. Even if we could know that a baby is going to die — isn't it our duty to do the best we can for her? I don't care if I'm being rude. I am disgusted by you. I can't even imagine what kind of person you could be to think that way. You claim to help people, but you don't have any compassion in your heart! I'll take care of her by myself — I don't want to have to ask someone like you for help ever again!"

My outburst must have frightened the baby because she started crying in my arms. I did not want to spend another minute in such a despicable place, so I carried the baby all the way home to my uncle's house without looking back.

The baby must have been desperately hungry, so as soon as I arrived back at the house, I soaked a cloth in sugar water and held her so she could suck on it. Then I gently laid her down on my bed. Unsure what to do for her, wondering about her parents, I found myself completely exhausted from the day's strain and decided the best thing I could do for both of us was to rest down with her.

I awoke to the sensation of my uncle tapping me on the shoulder. As I was sleeping, my uncle had gently placed a towel over her as a blanket. My uncle said quietly, "Sada-chan, the poor baby is dead." Even though I had known all along that the baby had little chance of survival, I was still heartbroken. It had happened so fast. One minute I was holding the baby in my arms, protecting her as much as I could from the cruelty of the world; the next minute, she was in Heaven.

I was so stunned that the tears would not come. I stayed awake all night and stared at the cold child. I could not stop thinking about the heartless man at the Japanese Red Cross. She had ended up dying, as he had predicted. I was filled with frustration — I wanted so badly for this mean and cold man to be proven wrong. I wanted to somehow show the value of giving this child compassion and love, and that by doing so, a miracle would happen and the child would survive.

A wave of depression came over me as I grieved not only for the baby, but also for the fragility of life. *Is it fair that human existence is so fragile? Why do we suffer so?*

But no matter how difficult it is, how deeply I am grieving, how alone I feel, and no matter how terrible I feel, I have to continue. There is no other option.

As the sun began to rise in the early hours of the morning, I remembered my anguish as my brothers left home to fight. I also remember my mother's face lined with pain, loneliness, and sorrow, trying patiently to wait for their return.

Yet another day had passed and I felt a lump in my throat as I also thought of my niece and nephew out there, somewhere, alone, without their family. I felt wretched and miserable. When I was growing up, I heard vaguely of the devastation of war, and discussed it in the classroom and read about in books, but I had never felt threatened by it on a personal level — it was always happening to somebody else, never to me. Now that was no longer the case. War had encroached upon our hearts and our lives, and there was no escape.

Waiting at the Foot of the Bridge

Morning, August 12, 1945

That morning, as I made preparations for yet another day of searching, I attempted to mend my torn sneaker. Even though it was still very early, the temperature was already scorching hot. I told my uncle, who was sitting with me in the kitchen, that I was beginning to give up hope of ever finding my brother's children, and questioned the value of continuing the search.

My uncle gave some thought to what I had said before he replied. "I understand your frustration, Sadako, I do. But think about it another way. In the same way that you have brought back injured children to this house to care for them, someone may be caring for your niece and nephew. If that is the case, it is each person's responsibility to help out whomever they can, whenever they can."

My uncle was right, of course. Even though I may not have achieved my original goal of finding my niece and nephew, maybe I was helping someone else's niece and nephew, and that thought gave me comfort. I was about to leave the house when I remembered that I had to pack my washcloth. My uncle insisted on giving me an injection of vitamin C from his pharmacy downstairs before I left. "You need all the help you can get," he said.

I began my journey and walked in the direction of where the electric railway tracks used to run. I was carrying my first-aid supplies and my lunch in the same bag, and as I was walking, it suddenly occurred to me that the unpleasant smell of the medicine might permeate the food.

My thoughts were abruptly interrupted by the sound of crying. "Please, someone, give me some water.... Some water... Water..." I looked around anxiously to identify the voice, but could not see where it was coming from. As I looked down to my feet, I saw a young woman crying, "Water... Water... My throat is burning. A fire is burning inside my chest. Water... Give me... water." I knelt down by the woman's side and poured drops of water into her mouth. She put both hands together as though in prayer. She stared into space for nearly five minutes and then opened her eyes wider and looked straight at me. Then she quietly closed her eyes, her head dropped to one side, and she died.

My certainty that I was doing the right thing by giving these poor people water gave way to doubt and anxiety as I watched this woman die before my very eyes. Although she was clearly desperate for water, and was in such excruciating agony that she cared little about staying alive, surely it was my responsibility to keep her alive for as long as possible. And that meant not giving her water.

I had witnessed so many people dying — the pain was almost too much to bear. I sat down on a stone and rested for a while. I had to figure out where to look next. The logical choice would be to head for the areas where I had not yet ventured, but yet again, my feet disobeyed me and turned in the direction of my older brother's house. In my head, I rationalized the change in plan by telling myself that I might come across some of my brother's neighbors while in the area, and they might have had heard something about my niece and nephew.

As I walked, I tried my best not to step on the corpses, but they were everywhere amongst the rubble from the fires that were still burning. Water was trickling out from the damaged water mains. I desperately wanted to freshen up, so I used some of the water to wash my hands and face and revive myself.

In the distance, I heard a dog howling. I looked around but could not see anything. At first I thought that I must have imagined the sounds, and that the stress of the day's events had taken its toll on my mind, but then, just as I was about to stop searching for the howling, I saw a shadow move in the remains of the wall of a nearby house. I ran over and saw to my horror that the dog was chained to an arm that was visible beneath the remnants. The dog was chained to her former owner and was unable to get loose.

My heart ached with sympathy for this poor creature. "You poor thing," I whispered. "Your Master is no longer able to take you for walks." I set the dog free, but instead of running free, she stayed close to her dead owner, licking his arm, as well as the wounds on her own paws. She showed no signs of wanting to leave his side, so I rested beside her for a bit, then stood up to continue my search.

I continued on my way and shivered in disgust as I passed once more the Japanese Red Cross station, recalling the previous day's events. I had to stop at the Takano Bridge to remove a loose rock that had once again found its way inside my shoe. As I stood up, I suddenly felt a wave of dizziness. The heat was so oppressive that I was starting to see double. I heard the voice of a young girl calling out behind me, saying, "Big Brother, Big Brother." I turned around and saw two young children with severe burns sitting on the ground, holding each other.

As I walked toward them, the boy deeply bowed his head. Very politely he asked, "Pardon me, but would you be so kind as to give my little sister some water?" Without hesitation I took out my canteen, and she opened her mouth with difficulty as I poured water in.

The boy seemed happy to see this. "Now, Midori, doesn't that feel better now?" he said as he stroked her hand softly.

The little boy explained to me that his sister had been howling all night long for water, crying out, "Water... Water... I want to drink some water.... My head hurts.... My body's on fire.... It's hot.... I feel sick.... I'm going to throw up.... Mother! Mother! Father... Big Brother..." The poor girl had not slept at all and he did not know what to do to help her.

I sat down on the ground and asked the boy to tell me about himself. Even though he was clearly in a great deal of pain, he was still eager to talk to me and tell me their story. He told me that he was in the fourth grade and that his little sister was five years old. Their family had recently moved here from Tokyo. Their father was a soldier, and they had no relatives and only a few acquaintances in Hiroshima.

"Where are your father and mother now?" I asked as gently as I could.

"A few days ago, Mother got a phone call from Father asking her to bring something to him, so she was away when the explosion took place. She hasn't come back home since. We were told in case of an emergency that we should wait here, but so far my father and mother have not come to meet us. We have been sleeping in the shade of this galvanized iron sheet."

Remembering my uncle's words about the importance of helping any child in need, I asked the boy if he and his sister would like to return home with me, but they both just shook their heads. I took out some small rice balls and dried sweet potatoes for the children to eat. The poor creatures had probably not eaten in days.

I placed a dried sweet potato in Midori-chan's hand, and she trembled and clasped it tightly as though she was afraid it would vanish. They both happily thanked me. I prayed in my heart that this food would help them survive.

After the sister had eaten two mouthfuls of the rice ball, she burst into tears once more, crying, "Big Brother... Big Brother..." I offered to hold her, and so she stopped crying, but her body was so burned that I was terrified that I would hurt her when I touched her. Nevertheless, I gently held her in my lap and she quietly closed her eyes.

But within a few moments, she found the energy to say, "Big Brother, Big Brother, don't eat all of it please! Let's save some for Mother."

"Don't worry, Midori," he said, "your Big Brother put away half of his for Mother, so you can eat without worrying.... It's OK." He tried to give her more to eat, but she seemed to have decided that she should save the rest of hers too.

I could not help but be moved by the children's evident display of love for each other and for their mother, who must have been very kind and helped them to learn how to care for each other. Since the beginning of my search for my niece and nephew, I had witnessed events horrific beyond imagination, but, at the same time, I had also observed the sweetness and compassion shown by so many young children whose instinct was to protect each other and their parents and grandparents. I suddenly felt embarrassed in front of them. If only adults would care for each other in the same way as Midori-chan and her brother, the world would not be at war.

Inspired by their devotion to each other, I was determined to help these children. I offered them more food to help them feel better and urged them again to return home with me. They were in serious need of medical attention and rest, and they could not get either by staying here. But the two were adamant that they would not leave this spot until their mother returned. Realizing that they would not change their minds, I told them that I would return the following day to see how they were.

"I will definitely come back tomorrow," I said, looking deep into their eyes, "but if by any chance your mother does return tonight, please tell her that you should all come to my house." I took out a pen and paper from my bag, drew a map with directions to my uncle's house, and handed it to them. "Well then, we'll see each other tomorrow, OK? Stay here until I come back, or until your mother brings you to my house." The brother and sister nodded their heads and promised me that they would.

I felt an overwhelming sense of foreboding as I looked at these two children. I tried my best to cover up my fear by saying to them cheerfully, "Well, shall we pinkie-swear that we will see each other soon?" I stuck out my two little fingers.

They both hesitated for a moment, but then stuck out their little fingers. As soon as I saw how badly their fingers were injured, I regretted my words. Their skin was literally stripped off from their wrists to their fingertips, and their bones appeared to be protruding. How could I possibly entwine those injured and pitiful fingers with mine without causing them even more pain? As I hesitated, the children stared into my face, their fingers reaching out to me.

Finally, I thought of what to do. "Since your fingers are burned, shall we seal our promise with our foreheads rather than doing a pinkie-swear?" I gently touched foreheads with Midori. "Did that hurt?" I asked, but she turned away and did not say anything. Then, I did the same with her big brother. When I asked him if it hurt, he also turned his head away from me. I tried to cheer them up and told them that we would definitely meet up tomorrow. When I stood up, though, they looked at me desolately.

"Well, Midori-chan, how about if I give you another hug?" Midori perked up instantly and happily stretched out both her arms. I delicately lifted her up into my arms, and gently stroked and kissed the top of her head. In response, she pressed her face into my chest. I then turned to the boy to say goodbye. "Big Brother, be brave. Remember, you're almost a man." As I placed my hands on his shoulders, he looked deep into my eyes.

I started walking, but every few seconds I turned around to look back at them. The boy was holding his little sister. I continued to look back until I could no longer see their figures.

I walked the streets, searching for my older brother's children, but my efforts were in vain; they were nowhere to be found. I was exhausted, body and soul. There was nothing for me to do but to return to my uncle's house. Today was no different from yesterday or the day before that. I was returning home without my niece and nephew, and they would spend yet another day alone without their family. My feet had become heavy and it took all of my willpower to drag them along as I walked home.

By the time I returned home, it was well into the day. My uncle was waiting for me and encouraged me to eat lunch even though I had no appetite. I told him the pitiful story of the brother and sister who were out there alone, waiting for me to return. My uncle insisted that I go back straight away and bring them back home, with or without their mother. My uncle ordered his housekeeper to accompany me this time — he did not want me to be out alone when I was so weak and tired. So just a half an hour after I had arrived home, I set out again, this time not alone, pushing a broken handcart.

While we were walking, I prayed in my heart that the children would still be there. After an hour's search, I found them lying on the ground, holding onto each other. I thanked God under my breath and, letting go of the cart, ran toward them.

The brother and sister appeared to have fallen asleep in each other's arms. As I drew near, though, I noticed that they were motionless. Shivers ran up and down my spine. I gently touched the boy's arm and stroked his forehead, but there was nothing I could do to shake him out of his sleep. I should have stayed with them longer. I just didn't realize they would die so soon. All the regret in the world, however, would not bring them back.

Who in the world started this war? Who committed this atrocity? Who allowed the war makers to inflict such suffering on pure and innocent children?

At that moment, the harsh words of the worker at the Red Cross reverberated in my mind, "This child is probably going to die, and even if it doesn't, what purpose does it serve in keeping a child like this alive?" There are those who think that children are far less valuable to this world than adults are, but I will never understand this way of thinking. To me, children are our hope for the future, and what could possibly be of greater value and importance than their existence?

My heart broke into tiny pieces when I saw that the little boy was still holding the half of a rice ball in his hand that he had been saving for his Mother. I sat down beside the two young dead bodies and burst out crying. I had known deep in my heart, when I had left the two children earlier that day, that something terrible would happen to them, but I was incapable of preventing this tragedy. My uncle's housekeeper gently suggested that perhaps we should head home. Seeing my hesitation, she added, "There is nothing you can do for these two, but you could still find your niece and nephew."

There was no point in staying here any longer; I stood up and once again said good-bye. Their faces were peaceful and calm, not revealing any of the horrors that they had endured during their short lives. The peace that suffused their faces seemed to be deeper than the sweetest sleep.

Maybe God, out of mercy, had already compassionately removed the pain and sorrow with which their poor little bodies and hearts had been filled. They must have been called to Heaven to be healed of their sorrow. But as much as I wanted to believe that was true, I could not convince myself that it was better that these children were no longer alive. *What is more precious than life itself?*

Bring Yuri-chan Too

Afternoon, August 12, 1945

Today was shaping up to be another pointless day. I trudged through the streets, calling out the names of my niece and nephew, but it seemed like there was little hope of ever finding them. As much as I tried to remind myself that I had to remain positive for their sake, the prospects of finding them alive were so bleak that I had trouble putting one leg in front of the other. I just wanted to go back to my home on the island.

I could not stop thinking about all of the children whose lives had been brutally ended. My head began to ache. I found a rock to sit on and surveyed my torn straw hat and the toes of my right foot that were exposed by a hole in my sneaker. The child in me wanted to cry out for my mother. I *had* to go home. At that moment, I made my mind up that it was time to leave Hiroshima. I had not found my niece and nephew, and all around me innocent people were suffering and dying. I was completely helpless. There was nothing I could do to stop their pain and save their lives.

I was halfway across the Miyuki Bridge when a woman hobbled toward me, holding a dead baby. "Please give me some water.... Some water... Water...," she begged. I quickly opened my canteen and was starting to pour water into the cap when she abruptly snatched it from my hand. I had not yet poured enough water for one mouthful.

When I took a closer look at the woman, my canteen fell to the ground. Her mouth, heavily bleeding, was torn to her ear. Her breathing was labored and the hand holding the cup was shaking. Blood had been oozing from her chest for some time. It had dried into thick, black clumps in places. I was so sickened that I could not say a word.

Though she had snatched the cup away from me, she did not make any move to drink the water. Instead she tried to give it to her dead baby. What was in her mind? Surely she realized that her baby was dead? Maggots were crawling over the dead baby's body, yet the mother continued to pour water into the baby's slightly opened mouth, even though it was running out the other side. She then looked at me and handed me the empty cup to be refilled. This time she drank it herself.

As soon as she had finished drinking the water, the woman asked me to help her put her child on her back for a piggyback ride. When I lifted up the corpse in my arms, its smell made me sick to my stomach. I was even more revolted by the maggots that had invaded her body. Once the child was on her back, the mother staggered off in the direction from which she had come. Even after the woman was out of sight, the putrid smell of her dead baby remained with me. I was more determined than ever to leave as quickly as possible.

When I had crossed the bridge and reached the area near the Monopoly Bureau, I came across a man and a woman who walked past me, almost falling over. A cute girl walked right up to the adults from the other side of the road. At first, I presumed that she must have known them, but the adults staggered past her without acknowledging her. More adults passed right by her, almost knocking the little girl to the ground. She started after them, but when I walked toward her, she ran toward me with both arms outstretched. She cried out, "Take me with you! Take me with you."

I put my arms around the little girl and asked her where she wanted me to take her. "Please, I want to go with you!" I asked her where her family was. "I don't have any," she said, clinging to me and sobbing.

"Well, let's go," I said, as she grasped my hand tightly. We set out, but after a while it occurred to me that the girl was probably hungry, so I asked her if she would like to sit down and have something to eat. She nodded her head eagerly. "Well," I said, "then let's do that. I'll make some room for us to sit down."

I kicked some debris to the side and cleared a space for us. I was just about to take a rice ball out of my bag when she asked me, "How about my older brother?"

"You have an older brother? Do you know where he is?"

"No," she said, her face falling.

My heart went out to this child. "Well, sit here beside me," I said softly. "We're already good friends, right? You can tell me anything." I must have reassured her because she sat down to share a rice ball with me. I did not press her to talk, but as she ate, she told me that her name was Yuri-chan and that she was four years old.

I gave Yuri-chan what was left of the green tea. She drew her tiny body up close to me and put both hands on my knees. It was amazing how much at ease we felt with each other, how close we felt. I could have held this little girl forever; she was so sweet that I wanted to protect her from any harm. I grew sad when I thought of this girl's family, scattered apart and lost to each other. Though not as visibly injured as many of the children I had come across, robbed of her family, this child, too, was a victim of war.

I asked Yuri-chan if she wanted more food, and she nodded. But she kept on sighing heavily, as if each bite she took was causing her pain. Once she had finished eating and we had rested for a while, I told her that I needed to apply medicine to her burns, and that she would need to be brave. Yuri-chan did not flinch during the treatment and waited patiently until it was over. "OK, it's time to go, little one," I told her as I put the medicine back in the bag. "Would you like me to give you a piggy-back ride?" I asked brightly.

She rewarded me with a wide smile, and as I carried her I sang a familiar song, "Sunset, Sun disappearing. The day comes to an end. The mountain temple..." She joined in, singing in a diminutive voice, "The bell is sounding. Hand in hand, let's go home together with the crows...."

As we walked along slowly in time with the music, gradually and without knowing why, we both started to cry. It couldn't be helped. I wanted to maintain a brave face for Yuri-chan, but deep sorrow overcame me. There could be no possible explanation for this suffering. A little girl had been separated from her family and she was now all alone in a harsh and cruel world.

When we arrived back at the house, I found my uncle resting, so I quietly went with Yuri-chan, who had fallen asleep on my back, up to my room. I gently laid her down on my bed. She began to stir, but as I softly fanned her, she slipped back into a peaceful sleep. I lay down beside her to get some sleep too.

I had just drifted off when Yuri-chan cried out, "Big Brother. Big Brother! Wait!" Startled, I jumped out of bed. I didn't know what to do, so I ran downstairs and woke my uncle. He watched her for several seconds, and then gravely shook his head.

"But her cry was so full of energy. Uncle, is there *nothing* we can do?" I asked him desperately.

My uncle replied, "I don't know if it will help, but take some absorbent cotton, soak it in water, and moisten her lips with it. Hold her hand, and look into her face so she can see you when she opens her eyes. Call out her name and keep talking to her."

I tried to follow my uncle's instructions, but I was paralyzed with fear and couldn't move. My heart was beating so wildly I couldn't think.

"Big Brother, wait for me. Big Brother..." Little by little, her voice started to fade. I felt so helpless and I started to panic. My uncle calmed me, urging me to keep talking to her.

I held her hand, took a deep breath, and called out, "Big Brother, come quickly. Yuri-chan is waiting. Come quickly." I kept calling out to him loudly, hoping that Yuri-chan would hear me. Yuri-chan opened her eyes and smiled. I squeezed her hand, and said in a soft but authoritative tone, "Wait until your Big Brother comes, OK? Don't worry, Yuri, he'll come."

She was too weak to form the words, but her lips said yes. Her eyes closed once again.

"Yuri-chan, Yuri-chan," I called out to her, trying to bring her back. Her eyes opened once more and she whispered, "Hold me. Please hold me."

I held her in my arms and kissed the top of her head. As she lay with her head pressed against my chest, waiting for her Big Brother, she quietly went to Heaven.

Even after Yuri-chan had stopped breathing, I held her tightly and did not let go of her. "Yuri-chan, you won't be lonely anymore. You'll be seeing your family in Heaven."

I felt so grateful that I had been there to take her home with me. Though yet another child had died, I was comforted by the thought that at least this little girl had not died alone, that she had passed over in my arms. In my mind, I conjured up the image of this little girl standing on the road all by herself while adults ignored her cries, adults perhaps too burnt and tortured themselves to respond. My heart ached as I recalled her angelic voice imploring just a few hours before, "Take me with you! Take me with you."

This child was killed even though she was not old enough to know the meaning of the word "war." I thought about all the other children whom I had met this week who did not survive, who would never see their families again. Through war, God had taught me how precious it was to live in peace. Perhaps this war was God's way of telling us Japanese that we have drifted so far from God's truth. As devastating as war is, I can only imagine that teaching us this lesson hurt God just as much, if not more, as it did us.

Enough! Stop the war! Why are we silent in the face of such horror and misery? I do not understand! So many lives destroyed over the last few years, and now this catastrophe has obliterated the entire city of Hiroshima. Tens of thousands slain as though they were insects, yet we still did not open our mouths in protest. Why do we let others deter us from shouting out to the world, "Stop the war!"? Why?

As Long as the War Ends, It's All Right If We Lose

August 13, 1945

Today marks the seventh day of my search for my niece and nephew. I have no idea where they could be. For all I know, they are already dead. I long to return to my mother, to my island; staying here seems pointless. But I owe it to my brother and, most importantly, to my niece and nephew to keep searching, no matter how difficult it is.

I felt disgusting and dirty, inside and out. I had not taken a bath in days and my face and body were caked with sweat and dirt. It's a good thing that I didn't have a mirror — if I looked half as bad as I felt, I would rather not see myself.

Last night was torturous. I could not get any sleep as sounds of crying disturbed my rest. The incessant weeping came from our next-door neighbor's children, who wailed, "Mother, Mother..." I wanted to see what was wrong, but I was so exhausted that I could not get up out of bed. When I woke up this morning, I decided to go over there and look in on the children.

When I came inside the house, I found the two boys sleeping on the floor on either side of their mother, their heads resting on her still chest. Their arms were wrapped around her body, clinging to her even in their sleep. I remembered my uncle telling me a couple of days before that the mother had been severely injured from the atomic bomb, and now it seemed that she had finally passed away. The children's father had sadly died in the war, and so the boys were now orphans.

I considered waking them up, but decided against it when I realized that the children had probably cried themselves to sleep. It was better that they have some rest, so I went back to my uncle's house to tell him what had happened. *War is abominable!*

I returned to their house an hour later to find that the older brother had already woken up. When he saw me, he buried his head in his mother's chest, clinging to her, crying and crying. "Mother... Mother...," he wailed.

Every fiber of my being wanted to join him in his crying, but I needed to be strong in order to really help them. Although I had the best intentions, my words came out so harshly that I regretted them as soon as they left my mouth. "Boys shouldn't cry. You are too old to be such a crybaby, you know," I told him. He looked at me in horror, so I added, "There are so many people — more than can be counted — whose fathers and mothers have passed away. What kind of world would it be if people spent all day and all night crying? Please stop crying now."

I tried to soften my tone and gently told the older brother what I thought we should do next. "I think it's best if we cremate your mother. If we leave her like this, she'll end up rotting. Surely that's not best? The three of us can burn your mother's body and turn it into ashes." I looked expectantly at him, hoping that he would realize that I was only trying to help.

He glared at me with eyes that were swollen from weeping. Perhaps it was too premature to talk about cremation, but a few minutes later, the boy assented. He then woke up his younger brother, Jun. Both of them were covered with such piteous burns that it was a miracle that they were still alive. I brought the two boys back to my house. It was a hard thing to ask them to share a normal meal in such circumstances, but somehow we got through breakfast.

After we had finished eating, we returned to their house and I removed one of their cellar doors, on top of which I laid their mother's body. We carried her on the makeshift bier to an open field out back and set fire to it. A crowd of people who were all too familiar with sorrow themselves had gathered in the field, also cremating their loved ones. Exhausted by sorrow and pain, the people abandoned themselves to grief as the bodies of their loved ones burned.

After the mother's cremation, at about eight o'clock in the morning, I left to continue my daily search for my nephew and niece, telling the boys that I would be back soon. I had seen so many corpses in the last several days that I was beginning to wonder what would be left of humanity by the end of all this. I was filled with grief and unbearable sadness.

As I passed by the Japanese Red Cross Hospital, I was shocked to hear someone call out my name. "Okuda-san!" I looked around, but didn't recognize anyone. I scanned all of the burned faces in front of me, hoping to identify the owner of the voice who had called out to me, but the charred faces were indistinguishable.

Several moments later, I heard my name being called out again and turned around to find a woman walking toward me. It was only after she told me her name that I knew who she was; her face had been so badly burned that she was unrecognizable. It turned out that she was a neighbor of my brother's. My heart beat wildly as I asked her if she had seen my niece and nephew, but she had not. She herself was look- ing for her two children and was hoping that I might have seen them. With heavy hearts, we embraced and wept, and then parted. There was no time to talk. Her children and my brother's children were still out there. What else was there to say?

Although I felt guilty for not focusing all of my energy on finding my niece and nephew, I could not stop thinking about my neighbor's children whom I had left behind that morning. I was anxious to return to them. In any event, I could not have continued searching for much longer, as my head was pounding from the lack of sleep the night be- fore. So yet again, I headed back. Before returning to my uncle's house, I went next door to check on the two boys and found them sleeping deeply under their window.

I woke up the boys and asked the older brother how he was feeling and if he had eaten anything. He slowly turned his head toward me and said drearily, "Only a little." The younger brother, however, didn't even raise his head to look at me. His eyes seemed to be open, but his body was limp. A sudden wave of nervousness hit me.

"Jun, how are you?" I asked the younger brother, with an edge in my voice, unable to hide my fear. "I bet you're hungry. Are you in pain? Where does it hurt the most? Would you like a hug?" Regardless of what I said, though, not one word left Jun's mouth. "Jun, try and get up. Please. I'll give you a hug," I said. Finally, he stirred and moved his arms slightly as he looked at me, but even this slight movement seemed to exhaust him.

I tried to reassure him. "You'll be OK before long. Just wait and see," I said. I lifted up little wounded Jun and gently placed him in my lap. His entire body was covered with wounds. I stroked his hair and sang to him. Jun was so weak that he no longer had the strength to sit upright. I knew deep down that this boy would not live much longer. A wave of misery washed over me and I protectively wrapped my arms even more tightly around him. I looked into little Jun's face and I rocked him slowly, back and forth, back and forth. He suddenly yawned, and as his mouth opened widely, it emitted a foul odor. I noticed with horror that the inside of his mouth was filled with blood that had turned dark red.

I asked Jun to open his mouth again for me. His older brother overheard me and asked anxiously, "Is something wrong? Is something the matter with the inside of Jun's mouth?" The older brother, overcome with an intense coughing fit, turned toward me and sought my hand. When I gently put my hand out, he took hold of it, and little by little, he drew closer.

"Jun, what's wrong?" the older brother asked. "Jun, please, just open your mouth and show me." However, the pleas of the older brother fell on ears unable to hear. Every now and then, Jun would yawn, allowing me with distress and bewilderment to look again into his mouth. Blood began to flow steadily from Jun's gums and throat. The odor was so revolting that I had to cover my nose to stop myself from vomiting.

"Did you see the inside of Jun's mouth?" asked the older brother. I nodded. "What is happening?" the older brother then asked me nervously. He took a deep breath and told me, "Just before my mother died, the inside of her mouth was also filled with blood. The smell was terrible. Does this mean that Jun is also going to die? There's no hope for him, is there?" The older brother then quietly closed his eyes and laid his head at my breast. Both lay in my arms, struggling to breathe.

I had no idea why Jun's mouth was bleeding the way it was, and so I shivered in fear. I thought that maybe my uncle would be able to explain the bleeding, so I carried Jun in my arms over to my uncle's, leaving his older brother behind for a short while. However, my uncle too was unable to explain the strange bleeding.

My uncle made some sugar water and brought it over to him, but it was already too late. Jun was dead. I bit my lip hard enough to draw blood and I felt rage and sadness rising in my throat. How could adults be so heartless toward children? Up until seven days ago, I had no idea what it meant to hate something so much that it consumed your entire being, but this is how I felt now about war.

I was so immersed in pain that I did not hear my uncle speaking to me. He came up to me and placed his hand on top of mine. "Sadako, I know how you feel, but right now there is a boy next door who needs you." My uncle's words brought me back to reality and I went back to their house, carrying little Jun's body in my arms. There was no way I could protect the boy from the pain of losing his younger brother, no way I could hide from him what had happened. I told Jun's brother to give his little brother one last hug, as I placed Jun's body in his arms. "Big Brother," I said, "please give Jun a hug. Jun, get a hug from Big Brother."

"When I smelled Jun's mouth, I knew he was going to die," he said forlornly. "There was no hope. Anyway, it's better this way.... I didn't want Jun to be left alone. This morning, there was a terrible taste in my own mouth. I began to wonder if my mouth too was beginning to have the strange bleeding. So I tried spitting to see if there was blood, and I realized that what happened to my mother was now happening to me. In the beginning, for Jun's sake, I would *not* allow myself to die, but now that he is gone, there is no point in being left all alone."

I fought back tears as I listened to the boy. His tone was one of resignation to his fate, rather than of anger or bitterness. He told me that he wanted to cremate his little brother before he himself died. "I'll place his ashes beside our mother's." With a sense of purpose, he carried his little brother's body out to the field. The fire was lit, as it had been that very morning to burn the boys' mother. Laying my hand on the older brother's shoulder, I prayed for some kind of healing and peace for this boy.

"Jun, Jun, you know your Big Brother will soon be following you," he said aloud. Unable to bear it any longer, I sat down on the ground and cried. I cried for Jun and his brother as well as the countless other victims whose lives were needlessly sacrificed.

Even as I cried, I knew he needed me to be strong, so I tried to wipe my tears and put my arms around Jun's brother. "Let's go home, shall we? Jun is now happy to be with your mother. He isn't suffering anymore. He's OK now."

In the circle of my arms, I could feel the boy shoot up suddenly, his body trembling. He yelled out, "You *Stupid* War! Give me back my father and mother and Jun! What did *I* do — what did any of us do to deserve this? Can you hear me? Say something!" The young boy spun in madness and screamed in defiance. There was nothing I could say in response.

My uncle, hearing the screams, rushed outside to see what was happening. He urged us, "Let's go home. Jun would not have wanted you to be so sad." My uncle lifted up the boy, who was holding his younger brother's ashes in his hand, and carried him back to the house. Even as he managed to calm us down, though, I heard him saying under his breath, "The whole world has gone mad to cause something like this to happen."

Once we were in the kitchen, my uncle requested that I prepare something special for dinner. Still holding the boy, he sat down and spoke softly. "You know, there are a lot of people like you who have lost their families." My uncle's glasses were fogged with tears as he continued, "You have to be strong, OK? You need to eat a lot so you can get more energy. You have to live a full life for both you and your brother."

For dinner, I made some miso soup with seaweed that I had been saving. My uncle and I were very careful to avoid the subject of war as the three of us sat together, instead trying to focus on the food. "Mmm. That's wonderful. Especially with the seaweed," my uncle said enthusiastically.

The boy commented, "*This* is my mother's favorite. If only she were here now...." Moved to tears, the boy put down his chopsticks and let his hands fall into his lap as the tears fell, teardrop by teardrop, onto the backs of his hands. "I'd like to offer her some..."

"That's a good idea," I said when I realized what he wanted. "Here — I'll get a bowl of the miso soup and we can offer it to your mother's spirit," ladling some into a rice bowl as I spoke. I then placed it in front of the old tin can that contained his mother's ashes — one of two holding the remains of his family. We gave ourselves up to crying as we struggled to finish dinner.

After we had finished eating, my uncle took me aside and said quietly, "You should sleep with him tonight, since he misses his family so."

The boy and I lined up our pillows side by side, and the boy fell into a deep sleep. I was so overwhelmed with misery that I was unable to sleep. When I looked at this young boy, my heart ached for my brother's missing children, who were about the same age.

The next morning, the boy asked my uncle, "Has the war ended? Japan probably lost, huh? It doesn't matter to me. As long as the war ends, it's all right if we lose."

Those were the young boy's last words.

Even Now the Memories of That Time

August 14, 1945

I wish somehow that the sorrow I'm surrounded by would no longer deepen. I just wish there would be peace again.

As usual, I left the house early in the morning while it was still relatively cool. As I searched the streets near my brother's house, I passed
a house that belonged to a woman I knew. I stopped for a minute as I
thought I heard someone call out my name. Standing at the side of this
house was a woman whose entire body was severely burned. As she
caught my eye, she started to walk toward me. I thought in horror that,
surely, this could not be the woman I knew? Tears streamed down her
charred cheeks as she cried out my name again. It was she.

We took each other's hands and cried. She told me that her daughter, Tomiko, was missing and that she had been looking for her day and
night, without any success. "When I first began my search," she said,
"I could think only of how I *had* to find my child, no matter what." She
began to lose hope of ever seeing Tomiko again.

"I know that I don't have much longer to live," she wept. "She's
probably already dead if I haven't been able to find her by now."

She asked about me and I told her about my ongoing search for my
niece and nephew, and that each day I hoped for a miracle, but as time

passed, I too was starting to give up hope. Even as we talked about this, our feet led us to continue together to search. We scoured all the shelters that had been set up, this time with renewed vigor since we were no longer alone and had each other, but still, no success. It was an almost impossible feat to find missing family and friends in the wake of the bomb. We may very well have seen our loved ones without recognizing them because of all the injuries. We talked about giving up for the day.

Noticing that the woman was out of breath and suffering from pain, I suggested that we sit down for a while to rest. It was then that she told me how she came to be separated from her daughter, Tomiko.

"Early the morning that the bomb was dropped, Tomiko complained of a headache and said that she wanted to take off from school. Her father, who is a soldier, was irritated with her for wanting to miss school, especially because that was the day when her class was assigned to help out in the war effort.[9] I remember his exact words to Tomiko, 'If you're *such* a weakling that you need to ask the teacher for a slightly easier job today, fine, but *you're going to school!* If you say such spineless things, Japan's going to end up losing the war.'"

The woman started breathing heavily. It was obvious that she was in a great deal of pain. Concerned, I told her that she did not need to tell me the rest of the story and that she would be better off conserving her energy, but she ignored me and continued.

"Tomiko is a good girl. She did not argue with her father. She got ready to go to school without even having breakfast. I was worried about her. I did not want her to have to go to school when she had such a bad headache, but there was nothing I could do."

"To make Tomiko feel better," the mother said, "I took out her *mompé* that matched my tunic and told her she could wear it to school that day. I had once taken an old kimono of mine and turned it into *mompé* for her and a tunic for me."

I indeed remember seeing them in happier days wearing their *mompé* and tunic, and her mother wearing that kimono before it was transformed into these matching clothes. It had a dark blue and pink floral

---

9During the war, schoolchildren were assigned to perform tasks at nearby factories or tasks that would be brought to their schools for them to perform.

design on a pale gray background. I loved that pattern and the lovely colors.

The mother continued, "Tomiko happily put on her special *mompé* and went on her way. After a little while, however, she returned home and stood at the doorway of our kitchen looking miserable and so all alone. With a tearful voice, she said, 'Mother, I *really* don't want to go today.' When I asked why, she explained, 'The string on my *geta*[10] broke....'"

The woman paused and asked me if I knew about the old superstition that if the strap of your *geta* breaks, something bad would happen. When I nodded, she carried on with her story.

"Well, I remember the pinched and frightened expression on Ton-chan's face as she stood cowering in the kitchen that morning. She was terrified of her father finding out that she had not gone to school after all. I needed to act quickly before my husband came home. I didn't have any other shoes, so I brought out for her my black *zori*[11] that I only wore to funerals, and I told her to wear those instead. Tomiko protested, 'These? You want me to wear these *zori* of yours? They're only for funerals — I'd be embarrassed to wear them — I don't want them. Get me some other ones, Mother.' Eventually, though, I convinced her to wear them and she left for school."

"As I stood in the kitchen doorway and watched her go, there was the blinding flash and explosion. I was sent flying.

"I had been knocked senseless, and when I regained consciousness, I found myself lying under the eaves of a house four doors down from our home. When I realized where I was, I picked myself up and hurried back to my house. My first instinct was to get to my youngest one. I called out to my son, who had been playing in the water in the bathroom when the explosion took place. 'Sei-chan, Sei-chan, Sei...' Not even a whimper greeted me. His crushed body was barely visible under the layers of debris. I wanted to dig Sei-chan's body out. However, the homes on our street were collapsing one after another, the fire breath-

---

10*Geta* are wooden platform thongs designed to allow the wearer's feet to stay dry walking through the frequent puddles caused by summer rainstorms.
11 *Zori* are a type of dressy thongs.

ing swiftly down the rows of houses. I left Sei-chan's body as it was and stumbled out of our house."

As she spoke, her face was filled with the type of anguish that only a mother who had lost her child could know.

"I searched everywhere for Tomiko-chan. I did not stop at any point to eat or drink — I had to find my daughter. Nothing else mattered. Even though I was suffering from terrible burns, I was not even aware of the pain. There were times at night when I would fall down in the road and lie there until morning came."

She continued to describe her search for her daughter, then she suddenly stopped. The strangest expression came over her face as she fixed her gaze on a girl who was passing by. I was worried that my friend was about to faint. She then whispered, "It can't be true. It's a miracle." Then she started shouting at the top of her voice, "It is true! Tomiko, there you are! It is you! You are wearing the *mompé* I made! It's Tomiko! Tomiko-chan!"

It is almost impossible to describe in words how full of joy Ton-chan's mother was at this moment. She swept her daughter into her arms, and cried, "Tomiko, it's your mother! Tomiko, you stayed alive for me! Thank God. Tomiko... Ton-chan..."

But Ton-chan did not recognize her mother at all and looked at her with confusion. She may as well have been hugging a complete stranger. When Ton-chan looked at me, however, a glint of recognition spread across her face. She said, "*You* know my mother! Please bring her to me! I beg you, Miss Sadako."

"Tomiko! I *am* your mother!" she pleaded, heartbroken. "Surely you recognize me?"

But Ton-chan continued to look at this woman with wary eyes. Though she was indeed in her mother's arms, Ton-chan just kept saying over and over again, "Miss Sadako, Miss Sadako, I'm asking you, please help me find her!" I watched Ton-chan's mother fall to the ground in misery as her daughter refused to acknowledge her.

I couldn't understand what was happening.

I gripped Ton-chan's shoulder and looked at her directly in the eyes. "Ton-chan, this *is* your mother! Why can't you see that? Why are you turning away from her? Can't you see what you are doing to her?"

But I may as well not have spoken as Ton-chan insistently averted her gaze from her mother.

I felt a stab of pain as I took in the pitiful sight of Ton-chan's mother sobbing on the ground, "*Why* won't you call me 'Mother'? Why not, Tomiko? *Please*, Tomiko!"

I tried to think of some way I could help, and finally suggested to her mother, "Do you have anything which belongs to you that she will easily be able to identify as yours — a watch or a ring, perhaps?"

The mother thought about it for a little while and then hit upon an idea. "I do have something! I'll go bring it. If she sees it, she'll recognize it right away and know I'm her mother. Sadako, please, help me by making sure that Tomiko doesn't go anywhere until I come back."

I did not know what to say to her as thoughts of my niece and nephew weighed heavily on my mind. I meant to have been searching for them all this time, but how could I abandon Ton-chan and her mother after they had finally and miraculously been reunited? "If it's for about an hour..."

"I'll come back soon — soon," she replied quickly and went on her way, almost running.

Two hours passed and there was still no sign of Ton-chan's mother. In the meantime, Ton-chan's condition suddenly deteriorated. Her breathing became labored, her eyes started twitching, and dark blood came gushing out of her mouth.

"Ton-chan, you have to stay strong. Your mother will be back soon. Ton-chan, please, stay with me," I urged her as her eyes started to close. I shook her gently and she opened her eyes slightly.

"Big Sister Sadako," she replied, "if you see my mother, if you meet her..." Tomiko never got to finish her sentence. She said that much and then died.

I cried out to her spirit, "Ton-chan, stupid Ton-chan, *why* didn't you recognize your own mother? *Why* couldn't you at least have said 'Mother'? It makes no sense! I just don't understand." By now, I was sobbing uncontrollably. Just a few hours earlier, a miracle had occurred and a mother and daughter had been reunited, against all odds. But it was all for nothing. Tomiko was dead and her mother would die soon herself, broken-hearted.

Shortly after, I heard the woman's cry in the distance as she stumbled toward us, shouting "Tomiko! Look at this! I have something! Here is the tunic that goes with the *mompé* that you are wearing. Remember how we love wearing our matching outfits when we go for a walk together, you and I? How we treasure these matching clothes. This is my tunic! This proves that I *am* your mother!"

When she reached us, she put the tunic on over her torn clothes. I could not bear to watch this woman talk to her daughter as if she were still alive, waiting for her little girl to respond. I stood up and reached out to wrap my arm around her shoulder. I told her quietly that Ton-chan was no longer with us.

"What? You're lying — she's not dead!" she cried, naturally unable to handle the sudden news. Between my sobs, I told the mother that Ton-chan had spoken about her just before she died. Ton-chan's mother shook her head in disbelief and squatted down in her grief, curling up into a ball by her daughter's side. "Tomiko, why did you die?" she asked. "I brought you back the matching tunic. And now you can't even see it! You died without your mother, without even letting me hear you call me Mother once more!" With a handkerchief, the woman fulfilled her last maternal act for this child and gently wiped away the blood from around Ton-chan's mouth.

She then stood up, still in shock, and gazed at Ton-chan for a while. Then, without saying a word, she turned around, pulled off the tunic, and started to walk away. She still held the matching tunic in her hand, but it seemed forgotten as it dragged along the ground behind her. I could not say a word. I could not do anything but follow her with my gaze as she retreated into the distance.

Ton-chan, Ton-chan, *why* didn't you recognize your *Mother*?

Ton-chan recognized me, but she did not recognize the woman who had carried her in her womb, birthed her, and raised her. Now Ton-chan's mother was all alone with no reason to keep on living.

My mind traveled back to the time when I lived in the same neighborhood as Ton-chan's mother. I remembered when she was pregnant with Tomiko. She said, "If it's a boy, my husband will name him 'Sei,' but if it's a girl... I'd like to name her 'Tomiko.'"

Ton-chan's family lived just a few streets away from my elder brother's house and when I used to visit my brother's family, Ton-chan would often come to play. "Big Sister," she would say, "I've come to play with you."

One particular incident stuck out in my mind. One time, Ton-chan's mother came round to my brother's house while I was there and asked me to hold on to the key while she took her daughter out for a walk, in case her husband returned before she did.

I can see Ton-chan now in my mind — she was full of life as she skipped down the road and turned to wave to me after every few skips. I recall thinking how glorious it was to be so happy. I got up to go, but couldn't resist turning around to wave to her once again. I remember going back inside my brother's house and a few minutes later, there was a knock at the door. It was Ton-chan.

"Big Sister, come here just a little minute," she said.

"Ton-chan, did you forget something again? You are a master at forgetting things," I teased her. Her face turned red with embarrassment.

"That's not it," she said. "Just lend me your ear a minute." She stuck her face near mine. Then she whispered, "If you look closely at my mother, wouldn't you say that she is almost a beauty?"

"You came all the way back here to tell me that?" I asked.

"Yeah, that's right," she said, her eyes growing wider as she spoke. "When my friend's older sister came the other day, she said that about my mother. I really think it's true. Since my friends said it, too..."

"Not only is she almost a beauty," I whispered as if I was sharing a treasured secret with her, "but she is a splendid beauty. She's not just beautiful, but sweet-natured and intelligent as well."

When I said these words, Ton-chan rewarded me with a wide grin. I saw Ton-chan's mother waiting in front of our house. "I'm leaving," she called, trying to get Ton-chan to go. Ton-chan flashed me another smile and ran back to her mother. I watched the two as they went along hand in hand, Ton-chan skipping even more happily than before, without a care in the world. I remember thinking to myself then how blessed they were to have each other.

Perhaps there is nothing to this story, but in my mind it may explain why Ton-chan didn't recognize her mother. Ton-chan could only see her mother as beautiful. But her mother had been so badly disfigured by the atomic bomb that when I met her, I couldn't make out the face of the person I had known. Thus, it was likely that, in her little daughter's eyes, Ton-chan's mother was completely unrecognizable. (I was easy to recognize, though, since I had hardly been burned.)

Until that day, Ton-chan had loved and treasured her beautiful, sweet, and intelligent mother. She was Ton-chan's pride and joy. When Ton-chan first saw the wretched, pitiful figure who claimed to be her mother, her mind must have shut down in denial. This creature's entire body, which was visible underneath her tattered clothing, was covered with hideous burns. Charred skin dangled from her face, whole layers of skin were peeling off, and there was an empty space where her left ear used to be; little of her was left but bones. It must have been too much for Ton-chan to take in. This could not have been her beautiful mother. There must have been some mistake. That must be why Ton-chan averted her eyes.

Even now, though, I still don't understand why Ton-chan's mother walked away without looking one last time at her dead child. I often think back on what happened that day, but I will never know the truth. I never saw the mother again. Still, I recall her anguish as she finally understood that Ton-chan was dead, and how she stopped crying and just walked away in a daze, like a sleepwalker, holding the dangling tunic, without even saying a word to me, without even wanting to tend to her daughter's body.

There is only so much that a human being can endure, and perhaps the devastating shock of all that had happened so exceeded the woman's ability to cope that both her mind and body shut down in protest. I would like to think that this is why the two acted in the way that they did. Otherwise, I just can't fathom their behavior. This is the explanation that gives me peace and helps me make sense of what took place. I will never forget Ton-chan's young voice, full of excitement and happiness, as she said to me, "wouldn't you say that she is almost a beauty?"

And so Ton-chan and her mother died and were returned to the earth in the Hiroshima of those days.

Human behavior in the weeks and days before the end of the war cannot be analyzed by normal standards. Only when you see, hear, and touch the horrors of war up close can you fully grasp the extent of the devastation war causes. In those days, we were not able to think clearly. People all across Japan were swept up into the mass delusion and hysteria surrounding the war, succumbing to a form of insanity. The bamboo spears that we were supposed to use to fight the enemy and the poles which were supposed to have been used to carry buckets for extinguishing fires did us no good. In hindsight, how incredibly ridiculous it is that so much effort went into producing such useless weapons. Bamboo spears!

I sometimes worry what God must have been thinking, looking down on our stupidity. I can imagine God saying, "What *fools!*" Even though so many decades have passed since the end of the war, my mind is still occupied with such thoughts. In recent years, whenever I see people act in a similarly stupid way, I tremble in fear. I want to cover my eyes and plug my ears, but there is no escape.

Ton-chan, I will always remember you and your beautiful mother, how sweet you looked in your matching outfits. I can visualize your mother's sweet, smiling face, but from time to time, my mind also recalls her pitiful, burned face. That face also belonged to your mother.

Restoring Faith

After eight interminable days of searching for my niece and nephew, I decided that it was time to return to my island. It seemed that my niece and nephew were nowhere to be found, and there were people on my island, my mother in particular, who needed me and relied upon me. I owed it to them to leave Hiroshima City.

Although I knew that I was doing the right thing by leaving, I could not help but feel an overwhelming sense of failure. Not only had I failed my niece and nephew, but I had also failed my sister-in-law who was too badly injured to search for her own children and who relied upon me to bring them back to her. The fact that I was unable to do so brought me immense sorrow.

During my agonizing search, I witnessed first-hand the cruelty and ugliness of war as families were torn apart, children were orphaned, and human beings were reduced to shells of their former selves. In the wake of the bomb, human dignity had been shredded and I was just a helpless bystander. I like to think that I helped some innocent victims, but ultimately I was powerless to truly restore their dignity, reunite them with their lost ones, and save their lives.

As I made my preparations to return to my island, I was no longer the same Sadako who had left for Hiroshima eight days earlier. During my time in Hiroshima City, my eyes had unwillingly been opened up to the horrors of war, and as a consequence, my entire outlook on humanity and the universe had been drastically altered.

My faith in humanity was restored to some degree when, to my surprise, my elder brother's two children appeared at my uncle's home! By some miracle, my niece and nephew, Fuyo-chan and Yukiaki-chan, made it back on their own! They had seen the sign that I had put up in their old neighborhood, telling them that we were waiting for them at my uncle's. They were both covered with wounds, but they were alive! We held each other tightly and cried with joy.

Early on the day when the bomb was dropped on Hiroshima, they had left home and were on their way to visit a friend's farm in order to collect some potatoes. As they were riding the train, they heard the explosion. It knocked them unconscious. When they came to, they found that they had been thrown into a rice field. Though they wanted to return home, Hiroshima was a sea of fire and the prospect of venturing through the city was too terrifying. On the fourteenth of August, though, they were finally able to join some adults and walk back. When they got to their neighborhood, they saw the sign that I had put up directing them to my uncle's house.

So in spite of the fears I carried with me every day, in the end, they were able to find us, in part because of the sign I had left for them. If it were possible for my joy to be any greater, knowing that I had helped my family in this way brought me great happiness and relief. Yet there were other children, not so lucky, and there are other stories to be told of the days and months following the bomb.

But They Said They'd Only Be Gone One Night

As soon as we could gather our things, I took my niece and nephew and returned home to my island. My brother's wife followed us there a few days later, but she was so worn out that she soon ended up in the hospital.

I quickly found myself caught up in my work, teaching my students and giving them a bit of stability amid the events that swirled around us. Still, the grief I had experienced followed me back to my peaceful little island village. I carried it in my heart and, in particular, saw it reflected in the small remnant of a family who returned about the same time I did.

The little girl's name was Rumi and she and her uncle were waiting in my village when I got back, though not waiting for me.

Her story really began one day in 1944, a year before the war ended, at the time of the general evacuations from the areas of the city most in danger of being hit with conventional bombs. On that cold day, a little girl named Rumi-chan and her family were evacuated from Hiroshima City to the village where I lived with my mother. During the war, the government moved many people to rural areas which were thought to be safer than the major cities and less likely to be targeted. Perhaps the government was also hoping to reduce people's fears about the safety of their children.

My village, to which Rumi and her family were moved, was called Ocho Village. It was part of the community of Yutaka-Machi, which lies on Osaki-shimo Island in the beautiful Inland Sea. The village, which is surrounded by orchards of mandarin orange trees, had always been very peaceful, but by the final year of the war, conditions in the village had severely deteriorated. Many families who had been relocated to our village from Hiroshima City found it extremely difficult to adjust to life in our small village.

On the morning of August 5, 1945, Rumi-chan's mother and father had left by boat for a visit to Hiroshima, leaving their three year-old daughter in the care of her uncle. "Rumi, be a good girl," they said to her as they parted. "We'll only be gone for one night. We'll be back soon, OK?"

The following morning, August 6, 1945, Hiroshima City was devastated by the atomic bomb. Rumi-chan and her uncle waited anxiously in the village for her parents to return. But they didn't come back that day, the next day, or the day after, or even the day after that.

After three days, Rumi-chan's uncle decided that it was time for them to search for her parents in Hiroshima City. Her uncle carried Rumi-chan on his back as they searched the city for four days, unable to find them. Exhausted and broken hearted, Rumi-chan and her uncle left the devastated city and returned to the island.

Starting on the day she returned from Hiroshima (about the twelfth of August), Rumi-chan would go out day after day to the rocky shore to watch the boats arrive, waiting for her father and mother. After my eight days of searching for my niece and nephew in Hiroshima, I too returned home to Ocho Village. Now home, every day during my lunch break, and on the way to and from the school where I taught, I would see Rumi-chan's desolate, lonely little figure huddled up against the rocks. She stared at the ocean so longingly, and with such deep concentration, it was almost as if she was trying to will her parents to return with her gaze.

The poor thing. "Hi, Rumi-chan," I would say in the hope of starting a conversation with her. Each day she would look at me silently for a moment, then say, "But they said they'd only be gone one night...." No matter what I said to comfort her, she would not say another word. She just kept looking at me with deep and sorrowful eyes. I would always end up crying with her.

Rumi-chan became a permanent feature of the seashore, wearing her *mompé* with splashes of bright colors and a yellow ribbon in her hair. On rainy days, she would hold on tightly to a torn umbrella, small, but still big enough to shield her somewhat from the rain whipping off the waves. On windy days, a hand towel would be tied around her head like a scarf. Every day she would stare, sighing, at the horizon of the sea.

I remember one day bringing a small pillow for her to sit on, but she didn't move and continued to stare out to sea. She just muttered desolately to herself, as always, "But they said they'd only be gone one night!"

This sweet girl seemed to be determined each day to wait for her parents, however long it took. No matter what anybody said, she refused to leave the seashore until after the sun set. When evening came, her uncle would say, "Rumi, are you still here? Let's go home." She would let him carry her home on his shoulders.

One morning, about four days after she had returned to our island (around the sixteenth of August), Rumi-chan was holding the yellow ribbon in her hand instead of wearing it in her hair. In its place she wore a cute hat. I sat down beside her and I peeked at her face. Without saying anything, she gently removed the hat and looked at me. I gasped involuntarily. Rumi-chan's thick black hair was falling out, revealing her smooth, white scalp.

After I had a moment to recover from the shock, Rumi-chan spoke softly, "Uncle said, 'cause Rumi's hair got sick, from today I can't wear my ribbon and must wear this hat.' So I'm holding my ribbon in my hand. Rumi's mother made it. Rumi loves this ribbon."

My heart ached for this little girl; her face was filled with such sadness. "Tell you what," I said, trying to inject more cheerfulness and optimism into my voice than I felt, "when your hair gets well, I'll make you another ribbon. And when you wear them both, you'll look like a doll! But you have to promise me that you will eat lots of good food, so you could get well. OK?"

She smiled and said she would. Within minutes, though, her sweet smile evaporated as she stared intensely out into the ocean. With tears filling her eyes, she lamented, "But they said they'd only be gone one night...."

I could think of no way to make her feel better. She deserved more than being told they would be back soon, a lie she could see through even at her age. I certainly felt I could not promise her that her parents would return. It felt far more likely that Rumi-chan would never see them again. In spite of myself, I felt a wave of reproach toward her mother and father. Why don't you come back? You said you'd only be gone for one night. She's waiting so!

When I spoke to Rumi-chan's uncle about the situation, he confided in me. "It looks like there's no hope for her parents. I still haven't gotten any word from them. Taking Rumi with me to Hiroshima was a terrible mistake. I thought it would be best for her to be with me then, but I think I brought harm to her by having her with me in Hiroshima. I can hardly stand it. I can barely look at her without crying. If something happens to Rumi... If something happens to Rumi...."

Rumi-chan's uncle let his head drop to his chest and bit his lip trying to bear his sorrow over what had happened. I looked into the ocean, hoping that some words of comfort would come to me, but no words would come.

Hour after hour, she continued to stare at the ocean, longing for her father and mother to return. Every day she was there. And every day, as though she were hoping that I might have learned something new, she would say, "But, they said they'd only be gone one night." Trying to hold back the tears, she would then turn back to the sea.

When I saw her uncle one day (it must have been about the twentieth of August by then), he asked me the same unanswerable questions I had been asking myself. "How can I possibly tell Rumi that she may never see her parents again? She's only three years old! How can I help her to understand without breaking her poor little heart? Yesterday evening Rumi wouldn't even look at the food I prepared for her. The only words she says nowadays are, 'Uncle, they've stayed away so long.' As I struggled to find the words to tell her, she held out her little arms to me, and as I wrapped my arms around her, her eyes were overflowing with tears. I could only hold her and cry." As he spoke, he let his own tears spill down his disconsolate face, making no attempt to wipe them away.

The day after my conversation with Rumi's uncle, I felt so swamped with work that I did not have an opportunity to check on Rumi-chan. Nevertheless, the next day I hurried to the seashore to find Rumi-chan being held by her uncle. The two of them were staring at the ocean together, locked in each other's arms. I sat down beside her and was taken aback when I caught a glimpse of her face under her hat. It had barely been two days since I had last seen her, but her face and lips were now dry and rough.

"Rumi-chan," I said, taking her hand in mine, "it's so nice your uncle's wrapping his arms around you."

"When Rumi went potty, it was red," she responded solemnly, "so Uncle's holding me." As I tried to take in her words, she pressed her face into her uncle's chest. Shivers ran up and down my spine as I looked at this sweet and innocent child. Not only was her hair falling out, but she was also having bloody stools. My body tensed as I realized that Rumi-chan wouldn't live very much longer.

I wanted to fulfill my promise to Rumi as best I could, and so I told them I'd be back soon and quickly ran home. I searched my house until I found some red cloth to make into a ribbon. I hurriedly made one and ran back to the shore to give it to her.

I found Rumi tightly wrapped in her uncle's arms, his head leaning against hers. She had closed her eyes and was no longer looking toward the sea. I called out to her, afraid she could no longer hear me, "Rumi-chan! Guess what I brought? Here's a red ribbon I made to go with your yellow one."

Rumi opened her eyes slightly and stretched out her palm weakly. As she showed me her crumpled yellow ribbon, I said brightly, "Now you have two, what do you think?" She opened her eyes a little more and smiled. As she opened her mouth, I could see that her gums were bleeding heavily.

"Say thank you," her uncle gently prompted.

"A-ri-ga-to-o," she said in a broken and pained voice.

"Rumi, Rumi, you're your Uncle's treasure, you know. I love you, Rumi," he said, gently and lovingly stroking her rough face. Two days later, Rumi-chan was called to Heaven as she lay encircled in her uncle's arms, still waiting for the boat that had taken her parents out on the sea.

War always brings pain and sorrow, especially to those who are young and vulnerable. After Rumi-chan passed over, there were many days when I would see her uncle still sitting at the seashore, as his niece had done, with both hands in his pockets, staring vacantly at the ocean. When or where the uncle who had been living by himself had gone, no one knew. It must have been about six months later when I heard that Rumi-chan's uncle had joined his niece in Heaven.

Even today, I still weep when I picture in my mind Rumi-chan sitting alone on the rocky seashore, her life ending as she held onto her hope that her parents would return. Whenever I walk along the seashore, the pitiful words, "But they said they'd only be gone one night," ring in my ears and haunt my dreams.

The Spirits That Haunt Us All

At times when I see this record of Hiroshima, the people — the way they were then — come rushing before my eyes, their voices into my ears. I want to be able to say to the spirits, "You can rest in peace now because we won't make those mistakes again." I do not delude myself into thinking that my protest about the horrors of the war will make much difference in the world, but still, for the sake of Rumi-chan and countless other innocent victims, I cannot cease making my appeal.

Japan's astonishing postwar recovery has made it hard for many to imagine that such a vicious and bloody war ever occurred. But I cannot help but think that even today, some child is crying out from underneath a tall building in Hiroshima, her body crushed and her voice moaning in pain, "Mother, help me — It hurts! I want water!" Entire families and neighborhoods were extinguished like a flickering candle flame in a strong wind. There are still bones of loved ones that were never claimed, possibly because there were no surviving family members who could claim them. However much humanity strives to forget such horrors, one cannot erase from history the fact that over a hundred thousand lives were instantaneously extinguished by the explosions that occurred over Hiroshima and Nagasaki on August 6 and 9 of 1945.

By the time the new year arrived, 210,000 people had died as a result of these two bombs.

Sadako and a Thousand Cranes tells us of twelve-year-old Sadako Sasaki suffering the effects of leukemia a decade after the bomb. Believing that she would be cured if she folded a thousand origami paper cranes, she eventually died, too.

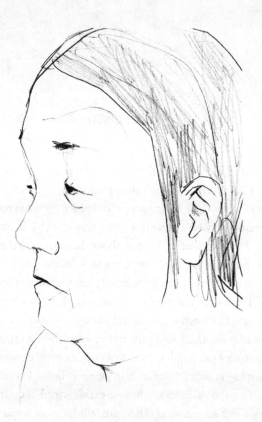

Even today, the putrid smell of burning corpses clings to my nostrils and chases me in my sleep. It is almost impossible to convey in words the gruesome images I witnessed and to impart the full extent of the cruelty of the atomic bomb. *We must never forget.*

For many years, I have been unable to give voice to my memories, but finally the time has come for me to keep my promise to those innocent souls that I was powerless to save, and to devote all my energy and attention to ensuring that such atrocities will never happen again. I want to teach the youth of today, who are thankfully unaware of atomic war, that nothing is more important than unity and peace and that there is never a justification for such cruelty.

In writing this account, my aim is to share these horrific memories with as many people as possible. My heart and soul continues to cry out for peace. It is my responsibility to do so because I have seen war with my own eyes and touched it with my hands. August 6, 1945 should be forever emblazoned in our memories as a day of repentance in which we recall the covenant we broke with God and banish all thoughts of hate. The destructive emotions of hatred and anger lead us to war. We can only achieve peace by each of us taking full responsibility for our actions and our thoughts.

The Years Before and After the Bombing

You may wonder what happened to me and my family in the years after the atomic bombing.[12] As you know now, the children of my elder brother Yasutami and his wife, Hanako, miraculously survived the atomic bomb and were reunited with their family. The son (my nephew) Yukiaki has since died, but the daughter (my niece), Fuyoko, is alive still. She married after the war and her husband is a priest at a shrine. Fuyoko herself became an elementary school teacher.

My life was forever shaped by what happened on August 6 that year — three days short of my 31st birthday. My life before the bombing was very normal for those days, perhaps in many ways like your life up until reading this book.

My Life Before the Bombing

I was born on August 9, 1914 in Ocho Village, part of the community of Yutaka-Machi, which lies on Osaki-shimo Island in Toyota County, Hiroshima prefecture, on the Inland Sea. My father, Tetsuji, was the chief priest at the Buddhist Temple Gomyo-ji, and my mother's name

---

12 This chapter is based on letters, emails, and phone exchanges with several of Okuda Sensei's (Teacher Okuda's) close friends, allowing us to better understand how the Okuda Sensei of 1945, a very special yet ordinary woman, was caught in the vice of world events.

was Ichi. I came from a large family of mostly boys, and being the first daughter to arrive, I was a tomboy and got more than my share of special attention. In my later years I was known by my students as Okuda Sensei (*Sensei* means teacher), but in my youth I was sometimes called Saa-chan, or "Daughter of the Temple," because of my father's position. Our neighbors loved me as the daughter of the temple, even after my father passed away from appendicitis at the age of 52.

During my childhood, I attended elementary school on the island for six years, but I went to live in the city of Hiroshima with my grandmother when it was time for junior high school. During summer vacations and winter breaks, however, I would return home to the island.

Upon graduation from junior high school, I entered *Yamanaka Kootoo Jo Gakkoo* (Yamanaka Girls' High School), a private high school for girls also in Hiroshima prefecture. I loved swimming and playing table tennis and basketball at school and sometimes defeated men in the games.

I graduated from high school in 1932 when I was 17. At around that time, I was diagnosed with tuberculosis and was hospitalized at a recovery center in Hokkaido for about six years. I also suffered from peritonitis, and the doctor and my family thought I would not survive. For a while, all I wanted was to go home and die with my family beside me. It is hard to imagine how thin and weak my body became. It was very difficult in those days to get someone well, even from just tuberculosis. Finally a doctor of acupuncture took on my case and treated me. He cured me completely and saved my life. He told me, though, that I could never have children and that I should never marry — that my body was too weak.

In any case, by the time I was well I was much older than the typical age at which women tended to marry in those days, and probably as a result of that I never found someone to marry, in spite of my fun nature and loving heart. And so I entered *Sapporo Gigei Senmon Gakkoo*, a vocational school in Hokkaido for sewing and handicrafts, graduating in 1937. For about eight years I then studied at Hokkaido Technical School, majoring in Home Economics. The clothes I created and my knitting were considered to be works of art, and some of my creations were shown in magazines.

THE WAR COMES TO AN END

I returned to my island village near Hiroshima City toward the end of the war and was living with my mother. My brothers had been sent to the front along with most of the local men, but the family of my brother Yasutami was still living in Hiroshima City. I was often called *Shima no Sensei* (Teacher of the Island) by the people in my village. This is how I came to be teaching knitting classes for children outside of Hiroshima City, when the atomic bomb was dropped.

On August 6, 1945, since our village was somewhat protected by the distance and the mountains between us and the center of the explosion, I was initially hurt in a way that was only slightly, if strangely, apparent. The people of the small island quickly sensed the almost complete devastation of Hiroshima. The decision my mother and I made to send me in search of my brother's family led to my further exposure to the radioactivity released by the atomic bomb. As a result, I lost all hearing in my right ear and lost much of my sight over the course of the next several decades.

LIFE AFTER THE WAR

After the war, I continued to live on my island, and in 1946 I entered Tachibana Dressmaker Women's School, graduating in 1949 from its course for teachers. In 1954 I again went back for further education, entering Sugino Dressmaker Women's School, graduating in 1957. In 1960, my dear teacher from Hiroshima, Hiro Masaike (now known as Hiro Suzuki, after her marriage to Sukeyoshi Suzuki), invited me to come and teach with her at the school she and her husband had founded, located in the region of Oguni in Yamagata Prefecture. It is here that I have spent most of my life.

The school, *Kirisutokyoo Dokuritsu Gakuen* (Christian Independence High School in English, or *Gakuen* for short), was founded in 1934 based on the ideas of the Nonchurch Movement (Mukyookai).[13] The Nonchurch Movement, founded by Kanzo Uchimura, has the perspective that Christian spiritual development may be enhanced without reliance

---

13 More information on this movement can be found in Caldarola, Carlo (1973) "Pacifism among Japanese Non-Church Christians," *Journal of the American Academy of Religion*, vol. 41, pp. 506-519.

on the structure of an organized church. The movement was influenced by Uchimura's early exposure to the faith and pacifism of the Society of Friends (Quakers). Sukeyoshi Suzuki was a disciple of Uchimura, and the school was created in response to Uchimura's dream of building an ideal Christian school. During the war, Suzuki was imprisoned for eight months for declaring openly that the war was immoral and that therefore Japan was destined for defeat.

I have until recently taught Home Economics (especially sewing, knitting, and clothing design) at the school and was the teacher in charge of the girls' dormitory. *Gakuen* became my home.

I brought with me to *Gakuen* the pages of the diary that I had written each night as I dragged myself across Hiroshima's desolate landscape in the days after the bomb. When it finally became possible, I turned them into the first edition of *Honogurai Tooshin o Kesu Koto Naku* (*A Dimly Burning Wick He Will Not Quench*), published in Japanese in 1979 by Kirisuto Shimbunsha (Christian Newspaper Company). I was so grateful for the help of Goro Makabe at the University of Niigata and to all those who prayed on my behalf as I tried to write the book, even with my busy schedule, deep in the mountains. Their assistance allowed me to tell these stories. I treasure the book they helped me create from the ragged pages of my diary.

In 1981, Sok-Hon Ham, the famous pacifist admired and loved by the Korean people, known as the "Gandhi of Korea," introduced my book to Korea. When the book was translated into Korean by Hyung Kyoon Cho, Mr. Ham wrote a heart-felt preface. This book was published in 1983 by Saenggaksa Publishing under the title *Kkojyo Kanun Tungpul Ul Kkuji Anko*. This was like a dream for me because I had long hoped that my book would be read by Koreans. I, together with the other employees and students of our school, have studied Korean. I prayed that God will bestow great blessings on the work of Mr. Cho and those who helped him. My heart was full of gladness and joy. Nothing would make me happier than if my small memoir could contribute toward peace.

A short time after my book's publication in Japanese I was asked by Tadao Miyamoto, a well-known illustrator of Japanese children's books, for my permission to illustrate two of the stories from my book.

We both wanted to transform these stories into picture books so that children as well as adults could learn what it means to use a nuclear weapon. The children's books we created were published in 1983 by Popura Publishing Company as part of a series called *Kodomo no Sekai* (The Children's World). The chapter, "The Big Brother and Little Sister Who Waited" became *Keiko-chan, Gomen Ne?* (Keiko-chan, Forgive Me?), and the chapter "But They Said They'd Only Be Gone One Night" became *Rumi-chan no Akai Ribon* (Rumi-chan's Red Ribbon). The text of both chapters was used unabridged for these children's books.

In addition to these print versions of this book, in 1982, as the children's books were in the process of being published, Nihon Terebi, a major Japanese broadcasting company, asked permission to produce a television broadcast about Hiroshima using the story from "The Big Brother and Little Sister Who Waited." This documentary combined interviews of me with the drawings from Mr. Miyamoto, as well as old footage of Hiroshima before and after the blast, and the music of the exceptional *Gakuen* student choruses.

It was in 1983 that I first met Pamela Wilson Vergun when she came to the school for a year to teach English. I am very glad that she is finally able to publish her edited version of my book in English, allowing it to reach a much wider audience.

When compared to many others who were exposed to the effects of the bomb, the physical effects I experienced were minor. The glass from the window near where I had been sitting left its mark in my skin; the molten fragment of glass blown out of the window burned into my neck. I also noticed immediate, though partial, damage to my right ear and eye. As I grew older, I gradually lost my hearing in that ear. My eyesight gradually worsened as well, first my right eye and eventually both eyes. I was also diagnosed with uterine cancer many years after the bombing, though treatment was successful. I did undergo eye surgery two years ago, since I was nearly blind, and so I'm glad to say that my eyesight has recovered a little bit.

My love of sports during my school years and my love of walking and hiking in the mountains all my life have rewarded me well, as my legs are strong. As my best friend, Hanako Sensei, with whom I taught at *Gakuen*, describes it, these days I live quietly at a retirement home, mending my clothes, helping prepare meals for others, and always knitting. I love having Hanako over. I enjoy it when she and the *Gakuen* choirs visit me. I send each of the students home with a hand-knitted wristband.

I am now 93 years old, living at the retirement home in the town of Oguni in Yamagata Prefecture, not far from my home of *Gakuen* in beautiful Kanomizu village, close to many of my dear friends. I hope that you will take up the cause I have carried and make it your own.

May the victims of the atomic bomb who lost their lives in our place find peace from the source of peace in the next world and may we carry out our lives in ways that honor their suffering. May we by our lives bring meaning to theirs that they may have not died in vain.

REMARKS BY A NOBEL PEACE PRIZE NOMINEE[14]

Sok-Hon Ham, Nonviolence and Human Rights Advocate
Translated by Soon-Won Park, PhD

February 4, 1982
A day when spring begins to burst forth

I was recently given a copy of *A Dimly Burning Wick*. I started to briefly glance through it before going to bed, but to my surprise I was soon completely absorbed in it and could not put it down. I have been to Hiroshima and have visited the horrible remains and relics in the museum. The feelings I experienced at that time, however, were no match for the moving emotions I experienced as I read this book. The true essence of what took place when the bomb was dropped is not adequately revealed by the relics and remains one finds in a museum. Through the eyes of Sadako Okuda, one can capture its spirit.

---

14 Sok-Hon Ham, the "Gandhi of Korea", was one of the most influential Asian leaders of the 20th century who advocated nonviolence and worked for human rights. He has been selected as a national cultural figure by the Republic of Korea and was twice nominated for the Nobel Peace Prize. This afterword by Sok-Hon Ham is excerpted from the original foreword to the first Korean Edition.

I marveled at the souls of the people I met in her book — at the way their minds were focused on helping each other. I cried with gratitude at the image of a burning wick dimly flickering, yet not quenched.

It was morning by the time I put down the book, all finished, and as I did so I felt drained and numb. I had a vision of the horrific, war-torn ground of Hiroshima, but then I had a vision of a small space between the deeply piled decaying corpses where a trembling new green leafy shoot emerged.

SADAKO'S EXPERIENCE AND THE INSIGHTS OF HISTORICAL RESEARCH AND SOCIAL PSYCHOLOGY

Pamela Vergun, PhD

In the presentations that follow, scholars discuss the decision to use the bomb and the reactions to that decision, both initial and continuing. They also foster an accurate and deeper understanding of why these events continue to be critical to the safety of the world. Because of my time spent reading, translating, and editing this book on Sadako Okuda's experience in Hiroshima, I have also developed insights about why her autobiography of eight days is so powerful.

Some of the information presented in the following discussions has always been available to the committed citizen-researcher, but the presentation of information about nuclear weapons has often been biased, as has people's understanding of what they hear. Other information comes from documents and other material that came to light several decades after the events, through declassification or other avenues.[15]

---

15 See, for example, Lifton, Robert and Greg Mitchell (1996) *Hiroshima in America: A Half Century of Denial*, Quill Press; Takaki, Ronald (1996) *Hiroshima: Why America Dropped the Atomic Bomb*, Back Bay Books reprint edition; Schaffer, Ronald (1988) *Wings of Judgment: American Bombing in World War II*, Oxford University Press; ABC News (1995) *Hiroshima: Why the Bomb Was Dropped*, Peter Jennings/ABC News Special, 2002 DVD release of August 27, 1995 broadcast.

The essays contained in this book will help to show why the decisions made in the 1940s are not the only ones that matter. The process of understanding history includes how we remember and use our history, and it should include a solid grasp of how social forces continue to encourage aggression. The goal is to facilitate a better understanding of how people across the world, individually and in groups, contribute to pushing the world closer to disasters like the atomic catastrophe Sadako experienced. This knowledge is also the key to enabling people to prevent disasters of many kinds.

Strategies such as using nuclear weapons against a country during wartime are typically the result of decisions made on a large political scale. However, they often have as great an impact on the individual level as on the global scale; arguably made for the "common good," we seldom see firsthand the damage and devastation of these large-scale decisions on an individual level. This disconnect between the global and individual allows decisions like the Hiroshima and Nagasaki bombing to be made again and again.

Since the 1940s, we have learned more about the range of threats to specific communities and the people of the entire world — the danger from nuclear power and weapons, and other human-caused threats — dangers we all share. We have also seen continued evidence of the inhumanity of even democratic governments — that sometimes intentionally harm people in pursuit of questionable goals.[16] In addition to threats that are clearly global in scope, there are other quality-of-life issues that first appear to only affect certain regions of the world or segments of society, but in reality have global implications as well. The events of 9/11 should have driven this home.[17]

---

16 Among many possible examples, one that stands out and which directly relates to nuclear weapons, is the experience of the Marshall Islanders. The ocean ecosystems and land (and the lives) of the Marshallese people have been used by the US as key testing grounds for nuclear weapons and intercontinental ballistic missiles in the post-Hiroshima world. Barker, Holly (2004) *Bravo for the Marshallese: Regaining Control in a Post-Nuclear, Post-Colonial World*, Wadsworth/Thomas Learning (Case Studies on Contemporary Social Issues). See also Horowitz, Adam (1991) *Home on the Range*, video documentary distributed by the Video Project on the use of Kwajalein atoll in the Republic of the Marshall Islands (RMI) as a missile testing site and the effects on the Marshallese people, land, and sea.

17 Paul Joseph, in his book *Peace Politics: The United States Between the Old and New World Orders*, addresses these types of effectively global threats: violations of human rights wherever they take place; politically repressive governments; poverty

The supporting chapters seek to demonstrate that we can develop a stronger ability to affect the world's course. Through improving people's intuitive understanding of this key event in history, and by increasing people's access to the social psychological research that shows us how social forces affect us, we can more effectively shape our future and that of the planet.

Sadako writes of horror and terror beyond most of our imaginations, yet the aspects of the stories that are most likely to engrave themselves upon our hearts are the moments of kindness, tenderness, love, and dedication to others. She shows us, for example, the often-hidden faces of older and not-so-old Japanese men who were loving grandfathers and uncles, who would struggle quietly against great odds to tenderly improve the lives of the small children in their care. She also conveys the insights of "mere" children who, relatively untouched by government propaganda and xenophobic fervor, focus on the universal sacred values of caring for one another, and by doing so sustain themselves. Perhaps that explains the relative peace that many of the children seem to have, against all odds.

Sadako's message is designed for *all* people, not merely those who feel confidently that war is never the solution. Perhaps it speaks most clearly to those who feel we sometimes need war as a tool in international affairs. Reading her account makes clearer why it is incumbent upon us, no matter how right the cause may be, to choose our weapons carefully. The stories of the children whom Sadako encounters raise the issue of personal responsibility versus collective responsibility. Who bears responsibility for something *like this*?

Sadako's personal sense of responsibility and guilt throughout the book becomes symbolic of our collective responsibility for the bombings. Her account reflects the feelings of guilt commonly felt by many who experienced Hiroshima.[18] Understanding how she and others were affected by these feelings conveys why her account is so powerful. Sadako was hurt directly by the blast when it blew a half-molten

---

whether in third world or in industrialized countries; and varying types and levels of despair among people throughout the world. These are all global threats. Joseph, Paul (1993) *Peace Politics: The United States Between the Old and New World Orders*, Temple University Press.

18 Lifton, Robert (1991) *Death in Life: Survivors of Hiroshima*, University of North Carolina Press (reissued).

piece of glass into her neck, yet she appeared unharmed relative to the horrendously injured people in whose midst she found herself the next day. She felt profoundly uncomfortable to appear so unharmed compared to those she encountered, a common indication of survivor guilt.

In a similar way, we, too, are subtly though deeply hurt by witnessing the pain of such people and are hurt by a fear of experiencing an event like Hiroshima ourselves. This fear and hurt are all the worse for Americans, whose nation was the perpetrator of the nuclear attack.[19]

In one of her many encounters, Sadako was quick to feel responsible for one child she felt she had killed through her stupidity (a sunshade she fashioned from the only materials at hand fell on the boy). Yet given how frail he must have been when she found him, most would objectively see the child's death as the result of the atomic bombing. Rescuers like Sadako typically feel they should have been able to save the person they were trying to rescue.

After the bombing, she regarded with wonderment the lies and propaganda to which she had acquiesced. She promised the children she met that she would try to tell the world how they suffered and how they held onto their kindness and humanity. Because of her experiences, her sense of personal responsibility is unusually strong. But I would argue that the voices she hears truly cry out for all of us to share communal responsibility for preventing such catastrophes.

There are many powerful ways we can act on this responsibility. History, sociology, psychology, and the work of other social thinkers can all help us to understand how actions are shaped by factors like flawed decision making, greed, and racism. The essay by Professor Ronald Takaki that follows, "A Lesson from Hiroshima," is immeasurable in helping us to understand the decision to drop the bombs on Hiroshima and Nagasaki, including the role of race. The article by Drs. Robert Vergun, Martin Donohoe, Catherine Thomasson, and me, "A Brief Summary of the Medical Impacts of Hiroshima," gives an overview of the human impacts of the bombing from a medical perspective, relating the medical research to what Okuda witnessed. The essay "Understanding Hiroshima — Personal and Policy Lessons to Take into the Future,"

---

19 Lifton, Robert and Greg Mitchell (1996) *Hiroshima in America: A Half Century of Denial*, Quill Press.

by Dr. Robert Vergun and me, describes how people make and justify decisions and how that affects the ways in which we remember history and create the future.

One small but significant contribution we all can make is to *pass on these memories* to others. As Professor Paul Joseph suggests in his essay that also follows, "Remembering Hiroshima," we can invoke the memory of Hiroshima in a way that makes it a much stronger symbol than it is now of the imperative for peace, and of individuals and nations joining together to prevent regional and international tragedy.

Remembering Hiroshima

Paul Joseph, PhD

Professor of Sociology, Director of the Peace and Justice Studies Program, Tufts University

Author of *Are Americans Becoming More Peaceful?* and *Peace Politics: The United States Between the Old and New World Orders*

Sadako Okuda's moving account of her experiences during the days after the crew of the Enola Gay dropped an atomic bomb on Hiroshima is important in many ways. The straightforward descriptions capture the impossible conditions that followed the detonation of the bomb.

Yet they also remind us that human beings retain an incredible capacity to survive and connect with each other even under the most arduous circumstances. Sadako continually asks why she deserves to live. But her heroic efforts to help the victims — sharing food, searching for family members, sharing medicine with strangers, and bringing them to shelter — serve as an eloquent answer to her own question. Her efforts to cope with a tragedy of epic proportions tell us that human beings can provide comfort and stand for a life of decency and peace even as the horror of war continues to cascade around them. Survivors are not only alive in the literal sense; their reassertion of humanity in the midst of terror serves as a special type of testimony: yes, war is terrible; but also, yes, human beings have the capacity to rise above it.

The memory of Hiroshima promoted by official Washington has attempted to obliterate both messages, namely that war is a tragedy for human beings and that human beings can actually stand up and prevent war. Instead, by attempting to keep the public insulated from horrific imagery, most US policy-makers have encouraged Americans to forget. Forgetting is a crucial act that requires as much organization, determination, and psychic energy as remembering.

Forgetting is rarely an accident. And official forgetting was initiated in the immediate aftermath of Hiroshima and Nagasaki. In the days that followed, a Japanese film crew documented the impact of the bombing on hospital buildings, transportation vehicles, rice fields, and, of course, on people. But the film was shipped to the United States, classified "Top Secret," and locked away for 22 years until it was finally pried loose. An "official" history, focusing on the alleged necessity of using the bomb to bring about the end of World War II, was quickly constructed, and the mythologies connected with that campaign also contributed to the process of forgetting the true reasons why the bomb was used.

For the entire Cold War period, indeed, even for the decade that followed, it has been the policy of the United States to rely on the threat to use nuclear weapons first. To remember the devastation of Hiroshima and Nagasaki, to tell a story, such as Sadako Okuda's, of what happened to a specific person or family, is to invite a human sensibility that weighs against that first-use policy. After all, a country that considers itself a moral leader cannot dwell upon the fact that it relies upon a security policy that targets innocent people. For Washington, nuclear weapons must remain distant and abstract. The more we remember, the more we know what happened under the mushroom cloud, the more difficult it becomes to live with nuclear weapons.

But forgetting Hiroshima — and Nagasaki as well — has not been the only response in the United States. On some level, Americans *do know* what happened there. I teach a class at Tufts University called "The Sociology of War and Peace." At the beginning of each semester, I ask my 50 students how many have ever seen photographs or films recording the devastation of Hiroshima and Nagasaki. Approximately, 75 percent answer in the affirmative. During the class, we view documentaries, watch videotaped interviews with *hibakusha*,[20] and review arguments among historians both in support and against the bomb. We also consider the behavior of the Japanese military on the Asian mainland and the debate within Japan over how that behavior should be represented in peace museums, history textbooks, and other public forums.

At the end of the course, I ask my students to complete the following sentence: "When I think of Hiroshima, I..." Few students choose to remember Hiroshima in a way that defends the use of atomic weapons. Most, thankfully, attempt to recognize the depth of the tragedy. Here is a sample of their replies: "I am struck with a feeling of deep hurt resonating inside." And, "Atomic bombs are ruthless: they desecrate land and the people." And again, "I cringe at the fact that our country initiated such an inhumane act. It disgusts me that we could ignore the fact that the Japanese are fellow human beings to the extent that we rationalized putting them through such torture and tragedy." And finally, "I feel something in the pit of my stomach that's hard to describe. It's regret, guilt, and disgust all combined. Somehow I feel my remorse or acknowledgement of the horrific circumstances is an act of respecting the experience." Here students demonstrate that they do have a memory. They recognize that Hiroshima is a central moment in our shared history. And it is important to note that the testimony of *hibakusha* such as Sadako Okuda is absolutely crucial in preserving that memory.

But there is another theme in the student responses that is perhaps equally important. They include: "Hiroshima is more difficult to approach and overcome because I feel helpless, without control, and unable to reverse or prevent the blatant power [of nuclear weapons]." And, "I think about many people's lives being destroyed and changed forever, and I feel sad for their pain and suffering, but yet I feel distant from it." And, finally, "When I think of Hiroshima, my mind goes blank. Such destruction is beyond my comprehension and thus my emotional

---

20 *Hibakusha* is the Japanese word used internationally to refer to nuclear victims, originally referring to the people affected by the atomic bombings of Hiroshima and Nagasaki, the "explosion-affected people."

bounds. While I can comprehend the death of a few, this is beyond me." Here we have another version of forgetting, one that is understandable even as it is also unfortunate. This forgetting reflects our limited capacity to hold the pain of others whom we do not know close to our hearts. This type of forgetting is also very different from official forgetting, or Washington's deliberate acts to promote the invisibility of Hiroshima.

These student responses suggest that it is possible for people to forget and to remember at the same time — and that it is also possible to remember in different ways. We can remember Hiroshima as an expression of evil, as a demonstration of the level of moral forfeit to which human beings can sink. We can remember Hiroshima as the site of important history lessons, such as the debate over whether "Little Boy" was the act that ended World War II or the fateful step that marked the beginning of the Cold War. And, along with Sadako Okuda, we can remember Hiroshima from the standpoint of the survivors: that the bomb was a tragedy of enormous proportions but also one from which it is possible to recover.

Her voice of hope and expectation in the midst of despair helps us see the possibility of using Hiroshima as a more universal symbol, as an icon whose memory inspires an ambitious arms control agenda with the ultimate goal of abolishing nuclear weapons. Throughout the world, people would use the memory of Hiroshima in their own local organizing against the particular examples of the nuclear establishment that happened to confront them. Those who opposed nuclear testing, military bases, the production of weapons-grade material, research and development connected to strategic modernization, or the deployment of weapons-systems would follow a path leading through Hiroshima and then back again to their own situation. Peace activists, those hoping to focus popular pressure so that their city council might go on record in support of nuclear abolition, or for a more strict commitment to non-proliferation measures, or for a new international nuclear weapons convention, would similarly enlist Hiroshima on behalf of their mobilizing efforts. Hiroshima could become a symbol of globalization that would be at least as powerful as the Nike swoosh mark or the golden arches of McDonalds.

We should recognize that over the past twenty years a policy of relying upon nuclear weapons for national security has partially lost its legitimacy, both among the public and among some segments of the policy-making elite. Former civilian decision-makers such as Robert McNamara, McGeorge Bundy, and George F. Kennan broke with nuclear orthodoxy in rejecting the first use of nuclear weapons and were later joined by retired generals and admirals such as George Lee Butler in calling for the abolition of nuclear weapons. In fact, I would argue that Americans are becoming more peaceful with regard to nuclear weapons, although too slowly and quietly to suit my tastes. I use the word "quietly" because there is, broadly speaking, little urgency on nuclear issues. It is possible that the need to forget about Hiroshima has in itself contributed to a broad "social numbing," a disconnect in US popular culture with both the past and the future. In addition, as a large continental power with a huge internal market and a privileged global position, the United States is a country that demonstrates comparatively little concern for history, especially the history of others. The economy is generally strong and most Americans are eager participants in a form of consumerism that provides yet another way of forgetting. The opposition to nuclear weapons that is so strong in some parts of the world is largely invisible to the American. An extraordinary number of Australian townships have placed themselves in favor of abolition. In New Zealand, opposition to nuclear weapons provides a point of popular consensus. Nor are Americans generally aware of such important developments as the Middle Powers Initiative or the International Court of Justice's finding that nuclear weapons are illegal.

Public opinion contains a paradox. A potential to endorse nuclear abolition exists but the arguments, powerful though they may be, that remain within the current terms of the nuclear debate will remain incomplete, their potential compromised. It is impossible to imagine abolition of nuclear weapons without public pressures. By themselves governments, especially the United States government, will never take the necessary steps. But the previously impossible might now be realistic. Public pressure for nuclear disarmament rests partly on creating a world where external threats begin to diminish and partly on regaining a sense that we can, in fact, control our destiny. For nuclear abolition to proceed, the world must appear safer. And the post September 11 world is moving in the opposite direction.

A reversal of direction is called for. While there are many steps, one of the most crucial is a constructive remembrance of Hiroshima. In fact, a basic familiarity with the facts of what happened in Hiroshima and Nagasaki, and what can be done to avoid its repetition, provide a litmus test, a kind of threshold in human literacy that caring people on the planet should recognize. As she wanders through the terror of Hiroshima, Sadako Okuda asked why she should live. As we read her powerful account of what happened, we should all be grateful that she did.

A Lesson from Hiroshima

Ronald Takaki, PhD
Historian and Professor of Ethnic Studies, University of California,
   Berkeley
Author of *Hiroshima: Why America Dropped the Atomic Bomb*

Let us begin with a fact: General Douglas MacArthur, Joint Chiefs of Staff chairman Admiral William Leahy, General Dwight D. Eisenhower, and Secretary of War Henry L. Stimson all believed that Japan had already lost the war before that fateful day of August 6, 1945, and that the dropping of the atomic bomb on Hiroshima was not a military necessity.

Why then did the president make the decision to drop the atomic bomb on Hiroshima?

Harry S. Truman was an accidental president. He had been sworn into office only months earlier, when Franklin D. Roosevelt suddenly died on April 12. Truman admitted to his wife that he had little knowledge of foreign policy. Feeling inadequate to fill the shoes of the great F.D.R., he had to face indignities and sarcasm. In the streets, people asked, "Harry who?" and mocked him as "the little man in the White House." But Truman hid his insecurity behind a façade of toughness.

Publicly, he presented himself as a man of the frontier. He blustered: "The buck stops here."

Many Americans were also swept into a rage for revenge for the surprise attack on Pearl Harbor. This rage had been racialized. Truman repeatedly blasted the enemy as the "Japs." In American society, this racist term identified the enemy as the Japanese people, a contrast to the term "Nazis" that indicated only the followers of Hitler. Truman also dehumanized the enemy in the Pacific war. Disturbed by Pearl Harbor and the Bataan death march, Truman argued: "When you have to deal with a beast you have to treat him as a beast."

These dynamics drove Truman to rigidly insist on unconditional surrender. In July, he refused to heed the recommendations of the Joint Chiefs of Staff and Secretary of War Stimson. They informed him that the Japanese government wanted to surrender but on a conditional basis — that Japan be allowed to keep the emperor system.

The top secret news of the successful test of the atomic bomb in New Mexico boosted Truman's confidence that he could bully Japan. In the Potsdam Declaration of July 26, Truman issued a fierce ultimatum: Japan must accept "unconditional surrender" or face "utter devastation."

Japan refused, and Truman ordered the atomic attack. The first bomb was dropped on Hiroshima on August 6. It was 8:15 in the morning, and Naoko Masuoka was on a school trip. She and her friends were singing about the cherry blossoms when she heard someone cry out: "A B-29!" "Even as this shout rang out in our ears," she recalled, "there was a blinding flash and I lost consciousness." Some 70,000 people were instantly incinerated to death. Most of them were women and children. Three days later, the second atomic bomb was dropped on Nagasaki.

But the Japanese government still refused to surrender unconditionally. At that point, Truman realized that his ultimatum had not worked. Changing his mind, he decided to allow Japan to surrender conditionally and to keep the emperor.

The day after the devastation of Nagasaki, Truman privately told a cabinet member that "the thought of wiping out another 100,000 people was too horrible," and that he did not like "the idea of killing all those kids." This was a feeling Truman would not acknowledge publicly for the rest of his life.

Secretary of War Stimson had written into the draft of the Potsdam Declaration a provision to allow Japan to surrender conditionally, with the retention of the emperor system. He was shocked to discover that that provision had been deleted by Truman in the final version. Had Truman left it in the Declaration, Japan might have surrendered before the atomic bomb was dropped on Hiroshima. But history did not turn out that way.

A Brief Summary of the Medical Impacts of Hiroshima[21]

Robert Vergun, PhD, Martin Donohoe, MD[22], Catherine Thomasson, MD[23], and Pamela Vergun, PhD

An estimated 140,000 people died in Hiroshima and 70,000 in Nagasaki by the end of 1945 as a result of the atomic bombs. Within the eight days Sadako Okuda spent searching for her niece and nephew immediately after the atomic explosion in Hiroshima, approximately 80,000 people died in that city.

The nuclear explosion created a fireball of superheated gas that emitted intense thermal radiation. At the hypocenter — the location

---

21 This summary was prepared in order to relate the research on medical impacts to the specific first-hand observations of Sadako Okuda and other *hibakusha*, and heavily draws upon: Committee for the Compilation of Materials on Damage Caused by the Atomic Bombs in Hiroshima and Nagasaki (1981) *Hiroshima and Nagasaki: The Physical, Medical, and Social Effects of the Atomic Bombings*, published in English by Hiroshima City and Nagasaki City (original Japanese report published in 1979 by Iwanami Shoten Publishers), pp. 30, 107, 113, 115, 118, 121, 126, 131-136, 140, 205. The eight-day mortality figure of 80,000 was estimated by Dr. Robert Vergun based upon the finding in this report that the number of deaths within each successive six-day period after the explosion decreased by approximately 50% (p. 107).

22 Martin Donohoe, MD, serves on the Board of Advisors of the Oregon chapter of Physicians for Social Responsibility and is the creator of Public Health and Social Justice.

23 Catherine Thomasson, MD, served as President of Physicians for Social Responsibility in 2007 and is active on the Board of Directors.

below the explosion of the atomic bomb over Hiroshima — ground temperatures reached 3,000 to 4,000 degrees Celsius (approximately 5,400 to 7,200 degrees Fahrenheit). This was roughly equivalent to 50% to 70% of the temperature at the sun's surface. The Hiroshima bomb released the equivalent of about 15 kilotons of TNT[24] and therefore most people close to the hypocenter were literally blown apart by the power of the blast. However, the vast majority of deaths in Hiroshima were related to thermal injuries as a result of the extreme heat of the bomb, complicated by suffocation as the firestorm consumed all available oxygen in the air.

The primary thermal injuries were flash burns, which appeared on areas of the body that were unprotected from the rays of the thermal radiation, for example areas not covered by clothing. The other type of thermal injuries or burns were secondary ones, so called because these were injuries that came about indirectly, for example, as a result of the fires spreading through the buildings of the city. Many victims were besieged by flames and had difficulty escaping from the buildings burning and collapsing all around them. Some were blinded by radiation or deafened by the pressures of the blast.

People and objects that were situated very close to ground zero were instantaneously vaporized. Near the hypocenter of the explosion, the heat radiation threw permanent shadows of the people and objects onto surfaces like sidewalks that had been behind them.[25] Many of the victims near the hypocenter in the central district who received severe thermal burns suffered loosened skin that fell off in flaps. In addition, a brief and sudden but extreme fall in air pressure near the hypocenter caused people's eyeballs to pop out of their bodies. Sadako Okuda describes these victims in her memoir.

Because of extensive burns and high fevers, victims begged and pleaded for water. This situation was made worse because of the difficulty of getting water after the bombing, coupled with the sweltering humid heat of even an ordinary Hiroshima August day. According to Sadako's account, as well as the accounts of other survivors, there were rumors circulating in Hiroshima following the blast that providing water to these victims would kill them. Most Japanese soldiers, medi-

---

24 Malik, John S. (1985) "The Yields of the Hiroshima and Nagasaki Nuclear Explosions," *Los Alamos Report*, LA-8819.

25 Liebow, Averill A. (1970) *Encounter with Disaster: A Medical Diary of Hiroshima, 1945*, W.W. Norton and Company, p. 124.

cal providers, and ordinary Hiroshima citizens did not understand the nature of the radiation and the injuries of the victims during the immediate hours and days following the blast. One possibility is that some people dissuaded others from providing water to the victims because of the belief that the ingestion of water would increase blood flow, which in turn would increase bleeding in these victims. While this may be the case, the most comprehensive and detailed compilation of the medical impacts of the atomic attack does not mention the consumption of water as a significant cause of acute death among Hiroshima victims.[26] Another possibility was the valid concern that the water itself was poisoned (by radiation, broken sewer systems, debris in the river), but the extent of many people's injuries was so great that poisoned water may not have hastened death by more than a few hours.

Many of the victims with thermal injuries also suffered crush injuries, lacerations (from shattered glass fragments, for example), bruises, and other wounds that failed to heal because of the harmful effects of the bomb's radioactivity on the body's immune and defense mechanisms. In particular, the radioactivity caused damage to bone marrow, suppressing not only the body's ability to produce white blood cells (leaving these immune-suppressed individuals extremely vulnerable to infection), but also suppressing platelet production (resulting in severe hemorrhage).

Deaths caused by infections that originated near broken, hemorrhaging skin were widespread in the days and weeks following the blast. Slow deaths caused by uncontrolled hemorrhaging in the mouth and pharynx areas were not uncommon, as Sadako Okuda witnessed.

Most health care professionals had been transported to the front and many who remained were killed or wounded in the blast. Thus, shortages of health care professionals, shortages of medicine, the destruction of transportation infrastructure and medical facilities, and pre-existing malnutrition from food shortages that existed in Hiroshima before the atomic bomb was dropped, all combined to greatly aggravate the situation. For the vast majority of victims, even palliative care with narcotics for pain relief was unavailable. The horror of

---

26 Committee for the Compilation of Materials on Damage Caused by the Atomic Bombs in Hiroshima and Nagasaki (1981) *Hiroshima and Nagasaki: The Physical, Medical, and Social Effects of the Atomic Bombings*, published in English by Hiroshima City and Nagasaki City (original Japanese report published in 1979 by Iwanami Shoten Publishers)

the devastation surrounding them surely must have compounded their final agonies.

Roughly 70% of Hiroshima's population that did not immediately die from the blast began to suffer nausea, vomiting, and/or lack of desire to eat within the first 24 hours. Radiation resulted in the death of cells (necrosis) throughout the body. Intestinal cell necrosis resulted in significant diarrhea in about 20% to 40% of the city's population. Gastrointestinal injuries generally impair the body's ability to absorb nutrients and therefore worsen the effects of malnutrition.

Among those who survived the first few weeks, 40% to 55% of Hiroshima victims began to experience hair falling out at the roots (epilation).

Ten to fifteen years after the explosion, almost one-fourth of survivors in Hiroshima developed cataracts. The most notable long-term impact, however, was the development of cancers.[27] Five to ten years after the explosion, doctors in Japan started seeing high rates of mortality from leukemia. Hiroshima and Nagasaki victims alive after five years who had experienced significant radiation exposure from the blast (equivalent to those less than 1.5 miles from the hypocenter) were about 50% more likely to die from leukemia compared to the general population in Japan.

Ten to fifteen years after the bombing there were high rates of mortality from other cancers (e.g., lung, stomach, liver, colon, bladder, thyroid, skin, multiple myeloma, breast, ovarian). Women who were 10 years old at the time of the blast and experienced significant radiation exposure were 25% more likely to die from cancers (other than leukemia) compared to non-exposed, age-matched women in the general population.

---

27 Committee for the Compilation of Materials on Damage Caused by the Atomic Bombs in Hiroshima and Nagasaki (1981), pp. 131, 218-219, 238-241. See also Pierce, D.A, Y. Shimizu, D.L. Preston, M. Vaeth, and K. Mabuchi (1996), "Studies of the Mortality of A-bomb Survivors: Part I (Cancer: 1950-1990)," *Radiation Research*, vol. 146, pp. 1-27; Thompson, D.E., K. Mabuchi, E. Ron, M. Soda, M. Tokunaga, S. Ochikubo, S. Sugimoto, T. Ikeda, M. Terasaki, S. Izumi, and D.L. Preston (1994), "Cancer Incidence in Atomic Bomb Survivors: Part II (Solid Tumors: 1958-1987)," *Radiation Research*, vol. 137, pp. S17-S67; Preston, D.L., S. Kusumi, M. Tomonaga, S. Izumi, E. Ron, A. Kuramoto, N. Kamada, H. Dohy, T. Matsuo, H. Nonaka, D.E. Thompson, M. Soda, and K. Mabuchi (1994), "Cancer Incidence in Atomic Bomb Survivors: Part III (Leukemia, Lymphoma and Multiple Myeloma: 1950-1987)," *Radiation Research*, vol. 137, pp. S68-S97. See also the web site of the Hiroshima Peace Museum, www.pcf.city.hiroshima.jp.

Among persons exposed *in utero*, about 25% who survived infancy suffered severe lifetime mental disabilities associated with abnormally small head circumferences (microcephaly).

All those who survived had a high risk of developing post-traumatic stress and other psychiatric illnesses. The costs of providing medical care and social services to victims of Hiroshima were borne by a Japanese economy weakened by the war.

Three days following the Hiroshima blast, a larger, 22 kiloton atomic bomb was dropped on Nagasaki, resulting in 70,000 deaths and similar short- and long-term health and societal consequences.

This summary cannot adequately survey all of the medical impacts of the atomic bombs dropped on Hiroshima and Nagasaki.[28] However, in discussing the historical, sociological, and political background surrounding the decision to drop the bomb, we should not lose sight of the magnitude of devastation seen in the raw numbers of people who were killed and injured in Hiroshima and Nagasaki. Furthermore, since we live in a world where the megatonnage of nuclear weapons vastly exceeds that of the Hiroshima and Nagasaki bombs combined, it is imperative that we work for peace and the abolition of these weapons of horrific suffering and mass destruction.

---

28 For example, it refers only very briefly to the mental health impacts on Hiroshima survivors. For more on those impacts, see Lifton, Robert (1991) *Death in Life: Survivors of Hiroshima*, University of North Carolina Press (reissued).

Understanding Hiroshima — Personal and Policy Lessons to Take into the Future

Pamela Vergun, PhD and Robert Vergun, PhD

The Background — Troubling Thoughts and Vocal Support

The justification for the use of atomic weapons on Japan in August 1945 is not as solid as some might like to believe. As historian Ronald Takaki mentions, all three military leaders at the time — General Dwight D. Eisenhower, General Douglas MacArthur, and Admiral William Leahy — believed that the use of the bomb was not necessary to end the war.[29] Takaki also notes that President Truman confessed privately after the destruction of Hiroshima and Nagasaki, "The thought of wiping out another 100,000 people was too horrible." Still, Truman announced repeatedly and unequivocally to the public that he did not regret the decision to drop the bomb, emphasizing the necessity of doing so on military and even humane grounds.

The Truman administration created a successful propaganda campaign to generate a mythology of the "benefits" of the decision to drop the bomb; this is one of the main points demonstrated by psycholo-

---

29 Takaki, Ronald (1996) *Hiroshima: Why America Dropped the Atomic Bomb*, Back Bay Books reprint edition, p. 32.

gist Robert Lifton and journalist Greg Mitchell in their 1995 book *Hiroshima in America: Fifty Years of Denial*. Lifton and Mitchell point out that this propaganda included lies such as the description of Hiroshima as an important Japanese army base in Truman's announcement of the bombing of Hiroshima. Another example of this propaganda campaign is how US Air Force Public Relations urged the American military to delay announcements of official estimates of the number of Japanese civilians killed, arguing that it would "make us look like barbarians." Air Force Public Relations made clear that the those estimates were to be released only after the US collected "atrocity stories about what Japs did to our B-29 crews when they were shot down."[30]

Moreover, detailed photographs and descriptions by journalists of Japanese patients in hospitals with hideous and never-before-seen injuries were suppressed by US military censors. It was not for an entire year following the bombing — after war correspondent John Hersey published his detailed accounts — that most Americans began reading about the physiological effects of the bomb, including death by radiation.[31] To counter growing reservations by the American public regarding the bomb after the publication of Hersey's account, the Truman administration orchestrated another wave of public relations efforts on the decision to use the bomb.

Social psychology suggests, however, that there are forces affecting public perceptions of the bomb that go beyond Lifton and Mitchell's argument about the effectiveness of the US government's propaganda campaign. In particular, there are social factors that allowed the US public to be susceptible to misinformation and less willing to consider information contradicting their predispositions. These factors quite possibly affected even the policy makers who were instrumental in the decision to drop the bomb, in the end leading them to believe some of their own misinformation — even Truman himself. In detailing these social psychological forces, this essays draws parallels between Truman's decision to drop the atomic bomb sixty years ago, and other decisions to engage in military conflicts, such as George W. Bush's decision to invade Iraq following the 9/11 terrorist attacks.

---

30 Sherry, Michael (1987) *The Rise of American Air Power*, Yale University Press, p. 346.
31 Hersey, John (1946) "Hiroshima," *The New Yorker*, August 31st issue.

The immediate reaction of policy makers and the American public following the use of the atomic bomb was strongly in favor of the use of atomic weapons on Japan. For example, after the second of the two bombs was dropped, Senator Richard Russell of Georgia pressed Truman to drop more.[32] Virtually all American newspaper editorials endorsed the use of the bomb. More than 50 percent of Americans that August approved of Truman's decision to drop the bomb on Hiroshima and Nagasaki (according to a Roper poll), while an additional 23 percent believed that many more bombs should have been dropped. Furthermore, 69 percent of Americans believed that the development of the atomic bomb was a "good thing" according to a Gallup poll; only 17 percent said it was a "bad thing", despite the fact that 27 percent of respondents *believed an atomic experiment would one day cause an explosion that would destroy the world.*[33]

Many Americans and others continue to have inaccurate knowledge of the history of why the bombs were used, and there remains a sizable portion of Americans who believe that the atomic bombing of Hiroshima and Nagasaki was justified. Marking the 50th anniversary of the bomb in 1995, the Smithsonian Institute planned an exhibit that did not merely present the conventional ethical and military justification for the decision to drop the bomb as though it were fact. This resulted in an uproar led by veterans groups, both houses of Congress, and several journalists that ended up forcing the exhibit to close down. More recently, in a 2005 Gallup poll conducted during the 60th anniversary of the bomb, 57 percent of Americans approved of its use in World War II, and in a similar Associated Press poll, approximately two thirds of Americans said that the use of the atomic bombs was unavoidable.

Behind the decisions made by Truman, military planners, and others since then, lay powerful forces that influenced their (and still influences our) judgment. Although these types of decisions are often framed in terms of "military strategy" and "imperatives," an understanding of sociology and social psychology allows us to more clearly see and understand the underlying forces that affect these types of decisions and ul-

32 Donovan, Robert (1996) *Conflict and Crisis: The Presidency of Harry S. Truman: 1945-1948,* University of Missouri Press reprint edition, p. 100.

33 Lifton, Robert and Greg Mitchell (1996) *Hiroshima in America: A Half Century of Denial,* Quill Press, p. 33.

timately impact American and world public opinion. These same forces also affect the interpretation of history and the actions that we take or fail to take to prevent further catastrophes — not only by Americans, but by people in all countries.

Conformity, prejudice, and the tendency to justify the use of militarily unnecessary and inhumane aggression in times of war are powerful social forces that have affected public opinion and policy decisions. *Understanding these connections is essential because similar social forces continue to impact beliefs and decisions by individuals and governments; we can use this knowledge to repair, rather than damage, the world.*

CONFORMITY AND MOMENTUM — NO TURNING BACK

Though Truman, as President of the United States, was the decision-maker primarily responsible for the first use of nuclear weapons, he only learned of the Manhattan Project — the name given to the secret effort by the United States to develop the atomic bomb and provide recommendations concerning its use — less than four months before that fateful August. When Roosevelt died suddenly in April 1945, Truman assumed the presidency and learned of the details of the Manhattan Project for the first time. Truman quickly accepted the presumption of key leaders on the Project that the bomb should be dropped on Japan.

Truman and others involved in the Manhattan Project conformed to pressure to go along with the plans already in motion. As General Leslie Groves, the Project's Director recalled, "Truman did not so much say 'yes' as not say 'no'. It would have indeed taken a lot of nerve to say 'no' at that time."[34] The scientists and technical specialists involved in the Manhattan Project were subject to conformity as well. As J. Robert Oppenheimer, the American lead scientist, described, "I did my job which was the job I was supposed to do. I was not in a policy-making position.... I would have done anything that I was asked to do...."[35]

Oppenheimer and the other scientists were also affected by their own version of the momentum, which was created by the rush to beat

---

34 Takaki, Ronald (1996) *Hiroshima: Why America Dropped the Atomic Bomb*, Back Bay Books reprint edition, p. 42.

35 Fieser, Louis (1964) *The Scientific Method: A Personal Account of Unusual Projects in War and Peace*, Reinhold Publishing, p. 14.

Nazi Germany at making a nuclear weapon. The bomb was originally designed to be used against Hitler, but after Germany surrendered, the people involved in the Manhattan Project kept on working. According to Oppenheimer, "When V-E Day came along [the day victory was declared in Europe], nobody slowed up one little bit.... It wasn't because we understood the significance against Japan. It was because the machinery had caught us in a trap and we were anxious to get this thing to go."[36]

In addition to the effect of conformity on the decision to drop the bomb, there were compelling though perhaps partially unconscious pressures on Truman and other decision-makers to justify the immense effort and government expenditures on the development of the bomb. In his announcement immediately after the bombing of Hiroshima, Truman proclaimed the development of the bomb was "the greatest achievement of organized science in history."[37] Indeed, the Manhattan Project was quite an expensive and difficult endeavor, described by one of the atomic scientists on the Project as "a formidable array of factories and laboratories — as large as the entire automobile industry of the United States at that date."[38] The Project produced a complex bureaucracy that, by the beginning of 1945, had required almost two billion dollars in federal expenditures.[39] The total expense was roughly enough to pay for the average annual cost of the *Works Progress Administration* (WPA), which for eight years and during much of the Great Depression financed and administered a series of popular New Deal projects that contributed significantly to the nation's infrastructure and arts. The enormous expenditures on the Manhattan Project — which, because of concerns for secrecy, were approved without even key congressional committees being aware of what was being developed — were in con-

---

36 Else, John, David Peoples, and Janet Peoples (1981) *The Day After Trinity: J. Robert Oppenheimer and the Atomic Bomb*, PTV Publications, pp. 14, 22. The trap mentioned by Oppenheimer is referred to by sociologists as "the technological imperative" — the tendency of many technological developments to create a strong presumption in favor of their use.

37 Takaki, Ronald (1996) *Hiroshima: Why America Dropped the Atomic Bomb*, Back Bay Books reprint edition, p. 6.

38 Goldschmidt, Bertrand (1964) *Atomic Adventure: The Political and Technical Aspects*, Pergamon Press.

39 Takaki, Ronald (1996) *Hiroshima: Why America Dropped the Atomic Bomb*, Back Bay Books reprint edition, p. 38.

trast to the very visible and beneficial impacts of other major federal expenditures such as the WPA.

Decision-makers involved with the Manhattan Project were concerned that there could easily be a public outcry if the bomb were, in the end, perceived to be unnecessary in the war effort. As the war against Germany was ending, Secretary of State James Byrnes worried that World War II could end before the Manhattan Project would be completed. He was particularly concerned over the public outrage that would erupt once the existence and cost of the Project became known.[40] General Groves feared that, if the war concluded without using the bomb, the expenditure on the Manhattan Project would result in "the greatest congressional investigation of all times."[41] When an undertaking such as the Manhattan Project is so costly, those involved tend to go to great lengths to rationalize their investment of time, energy, and resources.[42] There was great pressure on those in charge to find a way to justify the immense government expenditure and effort.

JUSTIFICATION AND COGNITIVE DISSONANCE

The pressure to justify the actions and results of the Manhattan Project influenced not only the decision to drop the bomb but the way history has been written. This type of pressure, ironically, stems from the fact that most people — presidents, military planners, and ordinary citizens — view themselves as rational and "good" people, and so feel pressure to act as though they are. When we commit ourselves to a course of action that requires considerable investment, we strive — mostly unconsciously — to make sure that our actions are consistent with this positive view of ourselves.

One way to cope with the discomfort that occurs when our actions do not match our view of ourselves as decent people is to revise our view of our actions — in other words, to feel that those hurt as a result

---

40 Lifton, Robert and Greg Mitchell (1996) *Hiroshima in America: A Half Century of Denial*, Quill Press, p. 6.

41 Ironically, in 1943 Senator Truman, as chair of a committee investigating wasteful war spending, grew suspicious of considerable and unexplained expenditures allocated toward the Manhattan Project. See Lifton, Robert and Greg Mitchell (1996) *Hiroshima in America: A Half Century of Denial*, Quill Press, pp. 122-127.

42 Aronson, Elliot (2003) *The Social Animal, Ninth Edition*, Worth Publishers, p. 177.

of our decisions *deserved* their fate, or at least that any consequences were somehow justifiable or unavoidable. This approach becomes especially tempting in the case of Hiroshima given the enormous consequences of this decision: the deaths of so many innocent children and a legacy of fear and danger for people throughout the world.

The discomfort caused by inconsistencies in how we think of ourselves and how we act leads to our attempt to restore our comfort by revising our own attitudes and beliefs about what we have done. Social psychologists call this process *cognitive dissonance*.[43] Once a difficult and controversial decision has been made — particularly if that decision is irrevocable — there is a deep need to come up with as strong a rationalization as possible in support of that decision. (The more reasons, and the stronger the reasons, the better.)

Because people tend to think of themselves as rational and good, there is a tendency to think about the decisions we have made as though they were consistent with being ethical and thoughtful people. Cognitive dissonance leads decision-makers, including presidents, to focus on the positive aspects of their decision and to downplay or even forget the less positive aspects when justifying their decisions.[44]

The pressure of cognitive dissonance can be extreme. Lifton and Mitchell demonstrate how this pressure has detrimentally affected Americans' view of themselves. The negative feelings experienced by Americans because the United States was the first to develop and use nuclear weapons has in turn led to negative behaviors as Americans have tried to grapple with the guilt associated with being the agents of such destruction:

> Americans were the perpetrators of Hiroshima rather than victims. Hence, the survivor struggle has been less that of the victim ("Why did I survive while others died?") than of the agent ("Why did we perform an act in which so many people, and in such a grotesque way, died?"). Even victims can struggle with feelings of guilt, but *perpetrators of such an event are likely to expend enormous*

---

43 For a discussion of cognitive dissonance, see Aronson, Elliot (2003) *The Social Animal, Ninth Edition*, Worth Publishers, as well as the seminal work of Festinger, Leon (1957) *A Theory of Cognitive Dissonance*, Stanford University Press.

44 For a discussion of presidential leadership and cognitive dissonance, see Lichtenberg, Judith (2007) "Presidential Dirty Hands," in Terry Price and J. Thomas Wren (eds.) *Presidential Leadership*, Palgrave Macmillan.

> *energy in fending off self-doubt. One can do that either by investing the event with virtue... or by seeking to divest oneself of the perpetrator's role....* [emphasis added.][45]

The psychological impact and effects on behavior of desiring and acquiring nuclear technology affect not only Americans but others throughout the world. We see this in the way countries and individuals frame their attempts to obtain nuclear weapons in such a way as to allow them to maintain their view of themselves as good and moral people.

Even when people merely create the conditions that foster poor or questionable decision making in others, they will likely justify their actions in less than ideal ways. Furthermore, people may cope with cognitive dissonance by turning on those who helped carry out their direct or implied orders, calling those who followed their orders "a few bad apples" and distancing themselves from the responsibility of creating "a badly constructed apple barrel."[46]

A careful analysis of Hiroshima and of the subsequent use, development, and testing of nuclear weapons shows that cognitive dissonance drove and continues to drive many aspects of the development and use of nuclear technology. When interviewed about the bombs, Truman made clear that he did not "waste a minute on regret" over his decision.

However, the strong desire of Truman — and of the country — to justify past decisions and actions has contributed to a distortion of history and continues to affect world views of the atomic bombings and atomic weapons ever since.

Cognitive Dissonance and the Search for the Highest Estimate

An example of selectively choosing facts to make a decision look good is illustrated in the conventional wisdom about how many lives

---

45 Lifton, Robert and Greg Mitchell (1996) *Hiroshima in America: A Half Century of Denial*, Quill Press, p. 208.

46 See Zimbardo, Philip (2007) *The Lucifer Effect: Understanding How Good People Turn Evil*, Random House; Tavris, Carol and Elliot Aronson (2007) *Mistakes Were Made (But Not by Me): Why We Justify Foolish Beliefs, Bad Decisions, and Hurtful Acts*, Harcourt Publishing.

were *saved* by the atomic bombings. The myth used as a key justification for dropping the atomic bombs on Hiroshima and Nagasaki — a myth still reprinted in American History textbooks and repeated by many Americans — is that using the bombs made a final invasion of the Japanese main islands unnecessary and so saved a million American lives. In other words, the bombings prevented the US from having to invade Japan and sacrifice the lives of American service personnel.[47]

The rationale that a million (or even half a million) lives were saved by using the bombs was never clearly supported by evidence. This has not, however, stopped it from being repeated as though it were an undisputed fact. Columnist George Will, in discussing the estimated one million lives that were "saved," argued that the bombing of Hiroshima was "a deed profoundly Machiavellian and moral."[48] The most recent edition of *The Complete Idiot's Guide to American History*, published in 2006, states that an invasion "was expected to add perhaps a million more deaths to the Allied toll."[49] Yet as Public Policy scholar Rufus Miles pointed out, "By the time historians were given access to the secret files necessary to examine this subject with care, the myth of huge numbers of American, British, and Japanese lives saved had already achieved the status of accepted history."[50]

The facts are these: In June 1945, the Joint Chiefs of Staff informed Truman of their estimate that *if* an invasion of the Japanese main islands turned out to be necessary, 25,000–46,000 American lives would be lost. General of the Army George Marshall and other military planners agreed that this would constitute a "relatively inexpensive" number of American casualties.[51] *So how did 25,000–46,000 turn into 1,000,000?*

---

47 This estimate is the most well-known one, made by former Secretary of War Henry Stimson in an influential 1947 *Harper's Magazine* article. See Stimson, Henry (1947) "The Decision to Use the Atomic Bomb," *Harper's Magazine*, February, pp. 97-107.

48 Lifton, Robert and Greg Mitchell (1996) *Hiroshima in America: A Half Century of Denial*, Quill Press, p. 269, originally quoted from Will, George F. (1985) "The Flight Of the Enola Gay," *Washington Post*, July 14.

49 Axelrod, Alan (2006) *The Complete Idiot's Guide to American History*, 4th Edition, Alpha Publishing, p. 268.

50 Miles, Rufus (1985) "Hiroshima: The Strange Myth of Half a Million American Lives Saved," *International Security*, vol. 10, p 121.

51 Lifton, Robert and Greg Mitchell (1996) *Hiroshima in America: A Half Century of Denial*, Quill Press, pp. 7, 27, 274; and Takaki, Ronald (1996) *Hiroshima: Why America Dropped the Atomic Bomb*, Back Bay Books reprint edition, p. 25.

According to Lifton and Mitchell, "the evidence is that no reputable military figure made such an estimate."[52]

It was not until 1947, in a highly popular and influential *Harper's Magazine* article authored by Secretary of War Henry Stimson, that a clear public statement was made by a member of the Truman administration on the number of American lives potentially saved.[53] Stimson's article argued that an invasion of Japan "might be expected to cost over a million casualties, in American forces alone." Truman's own estimate of the number of lives saved increased as time passed. After serving as president, Truman often cited his prevention of casualties, using an estimate of one-half million saved. Yet in the initial statements made by Truman announcing the bombing of Hiroshima, there was no mention of half a million American lives saved. In a letter written to his sister at that time, Truman provides an estimate of American losses that is 50% of what he claimed later, after his presidency.[54]

How did Secretary Stimson reach the estimate of 500,000 to 1,000,000 lives saved? A June 1945 memo provided to Truman from ex-President Herbert Hoover appears to be Stimson's primary source for the "documented" estimate.[55] At the time that this estimate was received by Truman, both General Marshall and the Joint Chiefs of Staff reviewed it and informed Stimson that the number was greatly inflated. Chief of Operations General Thomas T. Handy responded to it by noting, "It is obvious that peace would save lives and resources, but the estimated loss of 500,000 lives due to carrying the war to conclusion under our present plan of campaign is considered to be entirely

---

52 Lifton, Robert and Greg Mitchell (1996) *Hiroshima in America: A Half Century of Denial*, Quill Press, p. 180.

53 Stimson, Henry (1947) "The Decision to Use the Atomic Bomb," *Harper's Magazine*, February, pp. 97-107. Also, according to Lifton and Mitchell (p. 109), Stimson used the term "casualties," but policymakers and others citing Stimson's essay often misinterpreted this to mean "deaths," whereas "casualties" includes those killed and injured.

54 Truman, Margaret (1974) *Harry S. Truman*, William Morrow and Company, p. 6. Truman, in his 1955 memoirs, gave a figure of one half a million saved. See Truman, Harry S. (1955) *Memoirs, Volume I: Year of Decision*, Doubleday, p. 155.

55 Wyatt, Lee (1986) *Tainted Decision: The Atom Bomb and America's Rush To End World War II*, published by the Marine Corps Command and Staff College, Chapter 2, pp. 16-33; Giangreco, D.M. (1997) "Casualty Projections for the US Invasion of Japan, 1945-1946: Planning and Policy Implications," *Journal of Military History*, vol. 61, p. 541.

too high." Yet Truman and Stimson nonetheless continued to quote this estimate. Thus it seems that Truman and other American decision-makers gave into the temptation to exaggerate the military benefits of dropping the bomb on Hiroshima and Nagasaki, as social psychology would predict.

Regardless of whether estimates as high as one million were floating around, as one historian suggests,[56] it is telling that our accepted history has all but forgotten the existence of the more acceptable estimates presented to Truman by the Joint Chiefs of Staff, presumably the top and most knowledgeable military experts at the time. These lower estimates are overshadowed by statements commonly found in books on US history, such as in the most recent edition of *The Everything World War II Book*, published in 2007: "The use of such a bomb, *Truman's military advisors told him*, could help prevent the loss of up to 500,000 American servicemen should the Allies be forced to invade the Japanese mainland [emphasis added]."[57] This suggests a propensity of historians, policy makers, the media, and in part, therefore, the American public to selectively emphasize those "facts" that most strongly support the decision to use the atomic bomb. It would seem that Truman and Stimson, and many other Americans, found the higher numbers more reassuring as they contemplated the human and social costs of the atomic bombings of Hiroshima and Nagasaki.

AGGRESSION — THE MOVE TOWARD MAKING EVERYONE INTO ENEMY COMBATANTS

The domestic pressures described above converged with other social forces to drive the outcome toward using the bomb on the Japanese people. The years of war, accompanied by both photo and newsreel images of war, combined with patriotic movie films designed to keep support for the war strong, generated a numbing effect on the American public's response to the prosecution of the war. This played a role in people's use of and acquiescence to high levels of violence, eventually

---

56 Giangreco, D.M. (1997) "Casualty Projections for the US Invasion of Japan, 1945-1946: Planning and Policy Implications," *Journal of Military History*, vol. 61.

57 White, David and Daniel P. Murphy (2007) *The Everything World War II Book: People, Places, Battles, and All the Key Events, 2nd Edition*, F & W Publications, p. 159.

leading to a widespread resignation that "war is hell," and ultimately to an acceptance of the atomic bombing of civilians.

Ironically, but perhaps understandably, the horrible atrocities against civilians committed by Japanese and German forces during the war were a key part of the process by which the killing of innocent civilians gradually became easier to justify, even for those who had gotten into the war in part to stop fascism. Using every resource in the fight against fascism came to be accepted as necessary to end the violence of the war. Once people began to justify the use of excessive violence, it became easier to justify the use of even greater levels. Gradually, killing civilians had become easier for the US and many other countries. If people view themselves as ethical but at the same time grow accustomed to violence toward others, cognitive dissonance predicts that this inconsistency is likely to be explained away by convincing oneself that the violence is somehow deserved.

For example, in the first years of the war the Allies were committed to confining their attacks. But by February 1945 (six months prior to Hiroshima), American forces firebombed Dresden, Germany, killing several thousands of people, most of whom were civilians. Though this act was strongly criticized by some US officials, American forces firebombed Tokyo one month later, killing over 80,000 people, again mostly civilians. Brigadier General Bonner Fellers, an aide to General MacArthur, described the Tokyo bombings as "one of the most ruthless and barbaric killings of non-combatants in all history."[58] When the American public acquiesced to the bombing of civilians in Tokyo, it made the decision to go ahead with the deployment of the atomic bomb more likely to occur, since the precedent had already been set for attacks centered on civilian areas. Referring to the raids on Tokyo and other cities, Air Force General Curtis LeMay told a correspondent after the war, "I suppose if I had lost the war, I would have been tried as a war criminal. Fortunately, we were on the winning side."[59]

This process of acclimating the world, especially Americans, to using civilians as military targets continued inexorably. By the time the

58 Brigadier General Bonner Fellers quoted in Dower, John (1987) *War Without Mercy: Race and Power in the Pacific War*, Pantheon Press, p. 41.

59 Rhodes, Richard (1995) *Dark Sun: The Making of the Hydrogen Bomb*, Simon & Schuster, p. 21.

atomic bomb was dropped in August 1945, an American newspaper stated that the atomic bomb "differs in degree, but not in kind, from the other instruments of warfare in common use."[60] According to historian Ronald Schaffer, both Secretary of War Stimson and General LeMay argued, "the incendiary bombing [of Tokyo] had obliterated the barrier against mass air attacks on cities, making nuclear attack morally no worse than the Tokyo raid."[61]

This outcome, in which Hiroshima was seen as an acceptable military target for the atomic bomb, was facilitated in part by the shift in American attitudes toward accepting the largely indiscriminate killing of civilians that occurred in the last months of the war. Historian David Kennedy points out key differences in how the US conducted the war in Europe from how it conducted the war in Japan — and how this divergence in approaches was most noticeable particularly in the last few months of the war when Japan was the remaining enemy:

> In Europe the US B-17 and B-24 bomber fleets made a considerable effort to restrict their attacks to high-value economic and military targets. But in the endgame of the war against Japan, long-range B-29 bombers systematically undertook fire-bombing raids that consumed 66 of Japan's largest cities and killed as many as 900,000 civilians — many times the combined death tolls of Hiroshima and Nagasaki....The weapons that incinerated those two unfortunate cities represented a technological innovation with fearsome consequences for the future of humanity. But the US had already crossed a terrifying moral threshold when it *accepted the targeting of civilians as a legitimate instrument of warfare* [emphasis added.][62]

For the atomic bomb to seem like "just another weapon of war," and for Hiroshima and Nagasaki to be chosen as acceptable military targets for such a weapon, the US had to cross that moral threshold to the side where the mass killing, incinerating, and poisoning of civilians would be acceptable. Though American history has many instances of such cruelty, Americans' perception of themselves has often been that Americans are "the good guys" — Americans and their country are the "city upon a hill" — the leaders in the fight of good against evil. Faced

---

60 Quoted from the *Hartford Courant*. See Lifton, Robert and Greg Mitchell (1996) *Hiroshima in America: A Half Century of Denial*, Quill Press, p. 24.

61 Schaffer, Ronald (1988) *Wings of Judgment: American Bombing in World War II*, Oxford University Press, p. 175.

62 Kennedy, David (2005) "Crossing the Moral Threshold: Why US Leaders Never Questioned the Idea of Dropping the Bomb," *Time Magazine*, August 1, 2005, p. 50.

with the actions of Hitler and Nazi Germany and the other Axis powers, most Americans understandably felt that they were on the just side, and decades later World War II is still referred to as "the good war," one fought against powers that dragged civilians and neutral countries alike into peril. Given this self image, contemplating the use of an atomic bomb on a population center required first erasing the lines that had partially shielded noncombatants. This meant concluding that "they're all enemy combatants" — even and especially children.

The killing of children, *even those not yet born and those too young to speak* — had to come to be seen as acceptable or, to put it another way, as an unavoidable cost of victory. As Air Force Colonel Harry F. Cunningham put it, "We intend to seek out and destroy the enemy wherever he or she is, in the greatest possible numbers, in the shortest possible time. For us, THERE ARE NO CIVILIANS IN JAPAN."[63]

Americans want to see themselves as rational and decent. Yet even the slightest acceptance of unjustified violence against civilians throws this view into question. To lessen our discomfort we can come to the conclusion that the violence was unavoidable or otherwise justifiable. (For example, the Japanese use of children in manufacturing and the training of them for "homeland defense" were mentioned as reasons for the US military to treat them as combatants.) The easiest way, perhaps, to resolve this discomfort is to justify such killing by believing that the civilians, children included, deserved their fate.

PROPAGANDA — THE CONSTRUCTION AND MAINTENANCE OF PREJUDICE

Justification of our inhumane treatment of civilians often occurs through the rationalization that "enemy" civilians are somehow less deserving of human dignity than we are. Countries participating on both sides of World War II, including the United States, have had a long history of racism and hate crimes against groups of people both within and outside of their own countries. American newspapers, magazines, and comic books during World War II frequently depicted Japanese as not human. Historian Ronald Takaki argues that the war in the Pacific dif-

---

63 Colonel Harry F. Cunningham, quoted on p. 142 of Schaffer, Ronald (1988) *Wings of Judgment: American Bombing in World War II*, Oxford University Press.

fered from the struggle against Germany in that the enemy was "racialized" by Americans. Both Japan and America came to describe each other during the war primarily in terms of supposed racial difference, identifying each other's "race" as less than human and unworthy of respect. After the atomic bombings, American military leaders tried to understand and explain why Japanese civilians had sustained such hideous radioactive injuries from the bomb. Internalized racism, for example, led General Groves to ponder whether the Japanese people were somehow physiologically inferior, as he put it, whether there existed a "difference between Japanese blood and others."[64] This was easier to handle than facing the reality of radiation's impact on the human body.

The de-humanization of the enemy and shoring up of support for the use of the atomic bombs were aided by the suppression of available information about the bombs' effects. The American public was deliberately shielded from photographs of the injuries resulting from the bomb.[65] This concealing of evidence kept the focus of any discussions of the effects of the bombing that did occur on abstract numbers rather than on human beings. Thus the de-humanization of the enemy continued even after the war was over by keeping stories and pictures of those hurt hidden from the public. It allowed people to hold the impression that it was military personnel who were the casualties and avoided the more uncomfortable moral ground of allowing the experiences of particular civilians, including children, in Hiroshima to be heard. Film documentation of Hiroshima and Nagasaki and other nuclear tragedies was suppressed by the American military for several years. When the Associated Press did report shortly after Hiroshima eyewitness accounts of the injuries, editorials in

---

64 Schaffer, Ronald (1988) *Wings of Judgment: American Bombing in World War II*, Oxford University Press, p. 45. Eventually, Japanese victims were examined by American researchers to assess the effects of atomic radiation; the goal of providing medical care, however, was secondary. Shortly after this time, the US began atomic testing in the Marshall Islands, intentionally exposing the Marshallese to nuclear fallout from the blast in order to collect more data on the human impact of atomic radiation. The experiences of children and their families in Hiroshima, Nagasaki, and the Marshall Islands unfortunately are shared in part by people in the US, the areas of the former Soviet Union, and French Polynesia. The US, Soviet/Russian, and French governments exposed populations over which they had control, typically without the people's knowledge or consent. (The nuclear power accident at Chernobyl created a similar, though unintentional, exposure situation as well.) See, for example, Barker, Holly (2004) *Bravo for the Marshallese: Regaining Control in a Post-Nuclear, Post-Colonial World*, Wadsworth/Thomas Learning (Case Studies on Contemporary Social Issues), p. 121-139.

65 Lifton, Robert and Greg Mitchell (1996) *Hiroshima in America: A Half Century of Denial*, Quill Press, pp. 25, 57-61.

the *New York Times* implied that what readers had been told was Japanese propaganda. In the months after the bombing, even Truman was shown mostly aerial shots of the devastation.

Fifty years after the bomb, in the Smithsonian exhibit planned to commemorate the event, the tendency to avoid or deny the human effects was still at work, as "curators, under pressure, removed from the exhibit nearly every photograph of dead or badly injured Japanese civilians."[66] This effort to erase the visible and documented impact on humans has been thorough, successful, and has made it easier for the American public and others to accept the the feasibility of using nuclear weapons on a civilian population.

THE INFLUENCE OF COGNITIVE DISSONANCE — THE PAST AND FUTURE

Through using social psychology to gain a greater understanding of history, policy making, and our own decision making, we have seen the impact of key social and psychological forces. These forces — conformity, aggression, propaganda, prejudice, and cognitive dissonance — all affected the decision to drop the bomb.

Though today's international politics differ sharply from those of the world stage in 1945, the same social psychological forces are still actively affecting international affairs. When people or their governments seek to meet goals by any means deemed necessary, they will likely justify the actions by labeling their victims as less than human and somehow deserving of poor treatment. When we spend valuable resources on innovative weapons — or take actions that endanger our lives — we will often go to great lengths to justify the investments we have made and the risks we take. Decisions, including the decision to use force, are still made palatable through the use of conformity and racism, whether conscious or not. And once decisions are made, policy makers sometimes come up with "evidence" supporting those decisions and sometimes conceal or suppress evidence indicating a flawed decision.

This may well have taken place in the events leading to the US invasion of Iraq that began in March 2003. Prior to that invasion, and even before the terrorist attacks on the World Trade Center in September

---

66 Lifton, Robert and Greg Mitchell (1996) *Hiroshima in America: A Half Century of Denial*, Quill Press, p. xv.

2001, "hawks" within the Bush administration had spent effort planning and advancing the merits of an invasion of Iraq.[67] The American public was sold on the plan based largely on a claim that Iraq was developing weapons of mass destruction and on assertions of a link between Iraq and the 9/11 terrorists, although reports of evidence supporting this allegation proved to be false.[68] Yet after the US decision to invade Iraq — and well after the link between Iraq and the 9/11 terrorists was discredited — segments of the American electorate continue to believe the disinformation campaign advanced by the Bush administration. For example, a *Washington Post* poll taken six months after the invasion of Iraq showed that almost 70% of Americans believed there to be a direct link between that country and the destruction of the World Trade Center.[69] This clearly shows that the American public believed the propaganda claims tying Iraq to 9/11.[70] This also suggests, though, that the American public's uncritical belief in such claims reflected their underlying desire to be supportive of their government — to believe that their elected officials would not lie to them.

Understanding the role of cognitive dissonance can be useful in providing insight into the behavior of those you might oppose, such as the Japanese military during World War II, the German Nazi party, or modern-day terrorists. Although it is tempting to explain the actions of terrorists as those of purely evil and heartless people, they can be more usefully explained by cognitive dissonance. The underlying social concerns that foster terrorism may start out as reasonable goals such as reducing economic inequality. Yet if decisions are made to try to achieve those goals by any means necessary, the terrorists will be less constrained in their actions and then will be tempted to justify the atrocities they have committed.

The influence of cognitive dissonance continues to be powerful in today's events, even as it was during the atomic bombing of Hiroshima.

---

67 Woodward, Bob (2004) *Plan of Attack*, Simon & Schuster, p. 9.

68 See, for example, National Commission on Terrorist Attacks (2004) *The 9/11 Commission Report: Final Report of the National Commission on Terrorist Attacks Upon the United States*, W. W. Norton & Company (Authorized Edition), pp. 334-8.

69 Milbank, Dana and Claudia Deane (2003) "Hussein Link to 9/11 Lingers in Many Minds," *Washington Post*, September 6.

70 Public Broadcasting Service (2004) "Chasing Saddam's Weapons" *Frontline* (original broadcast: January 22, 2004).

As social psychologist Elliot Aronson notes, "If individuals concentrate their time and effort on protecting their egos, they will never grow. In order to grow, we must learn from our mistakes. But if we are intent on reducing dissonance, we will not admit to our mistakes. Instead, we will sweep them under the rug, or, worse still, we will turn them into virtues. The memoirs of former presidents are full of [these kinds] of self-serving, self-justifying statements."[71] Yet we would add, following in the footsteps of social psychologists Elliot Aronson and Philip Zimbardo, *equipped with the knowledge of how these dynamics work, we can resist them and more clearly see the past and protect the future.*

71 Aronson, Elliot (2003) *The Social Animal, Ninth Edition,* Worth Publishers, p. 198.

ACKNOWLEDGEMENTS

Twenty-four years ago I had the honor of meeting Sadako Teiko Okuda. Thank you, "Okuda Sensei," with all my heart; I wish I could deliver this to you in person. Thank you also, Hanako Masumoto, who knows best the heart of Okuda Sensei. Your support and your research have made an invaluable contribution to the clarity and future of this work.

I would like to thank Martin DeMers, Andrea Sengstacken, and the staff of Algora Publishing for taking on this project and allowing the world to learn from Hiroshima's past. Thank you, also, Mia Nolting, for your illustrations. It is no small task to illustrate a book about human-kind at its worst and best. I am very grateful to my contributors, Paul Joseph, Catherine Thomasson, and Ron Takaki, for your support that kept me going at difficult moments.

My deepest gratitude goes to my husband Robert Allen Vergun, who has worked tirelessly to get this book published and do the innu-merable things needed to make it strong. I am grateful for your brilliant research and writing talents, my companion and collaborator.

Beverly Bryant Blodgett Wilson and Frank Pereira Wilson — you are among our greatest blessings, and without you this book might never have come to press again. To my wonderful children. Miko Bev-erly Jimon-Clare Vergun and Isaac Brian Michael Vergun, you gave so much of our time together to make this book possible with amazing gracefulness. I love you with all my heart.

My brother, James Lee Wilson, lent his artistic talent to the book's illustrations, cover design, and website. Lawrence M. Vergun, Attorney at Law, rose to the occasion when his offer of help led to an invitation to become vitally involved in the final stages of creating, protecting, and publicizing this book.

Special thanks to Kent Calder, who made the first full draft of the translation possible, to Toshiko Calder who insured its initial accuracy, and to Mark Selden, through whose recommendation Okuda's memoir has forever been given even greater power.

Thank you, Toshisuke and Kazuko Konno, Mikako Matsumoto, Mitsuko and Nobu Sukegawa, Masahiro and Yumiko Goto, Mikihiko Kubo (one of Okuda's younger brothers), Joji Muramoto, Hyung Kyoon Cho (translator of the first Korean edition), Kyoko Shimomitsu, Shu-ichi and Yoko Taguchi, and Chami Nagai, for helping to increase the value and reach of this work not only for today's readers but for others in the future. A special thanks to Yasuko Tashiro for her translation of important documents with great care, helping inestimably in the last year. Thank you to renowned calligrapher Umeko Masumoto for her beautiful Japanese calligraphy of "A Dimly Burning Wick He Will Not Quench" that graces this book. Thank you to Jennifer Jung-Kim and John B. Duncan for kindly translating the afterwords from the original Korean edition into English, to Soon-Won Park for supportively translating the chapter by Ham, and to Martin Donohoe for his contributions to the medical chapter.

Diana Ramirez, Susie Wu, Anthony Floyd, Andrea Vergun, and Kelly and Jon Nutting made amazing contributions in editing and art direction and gave generously of their help, and Sorelle Weinstein was a great help with editing.

To the others whom I have not mentioned by name but who have provided encouragement, ideas, and suggestions, thank you so much. Working on a book about Hiroshima calls for a strong source of hope and renewal; we are grateful for everyone's support.

Peace and hope,
Pamela Bea Wilson Vergun

It is no longer a choice, my friends, between violence and nonviolence. It is either nonviolence or nonexistence. And the alternative to disarmament, the alternative to a greater suspension of nuclear tests, the alternative to strengthening the United Nations and thereby disarming the whole world, may well be a civilization plunged into the abyss of annihilation, and our earthly habitat would be transformed into an inferno that even the mind of Dante could not imagine.

— Martin Luther King, Jr., "Remaining Awake Through A Great Revolution", Sermon delivered March 31, 1968, at the National Cathedral, Washington, D.C., 11 pp.

More recently I have come to see the need for the method of nonviolence in international relations. Although I was not yet convinced of its efficacy in conflicts between nations, I felt that while war could never be a positive good, it could serve as a negative good by preventing the spread and growth of an evil force. War, horrible as it is, might be preferable to surrender to a totalitarian system. But now I believe that the potential destructiveness of modern weapons totally rules out the possibility of war ever again achieving a negative good. If we assume that mankind has a right to survive then we must find an alternative to war and destruction.

— Martin Luther King, Jr., "Pilgrimage to Nonviolence" in *Strength to Love* (1958)